WORDS MADE FLESH

Words Made Flesh

God Speaks to Us in the
Ordinary Things of Life

Harry Blamires

SERVANT BOOKS
Ann Arbor, Michigan

Available from
Servant Publications,
Box 8617,
Ann Arbor, Michigan 48107

ISBN 0-89283-235-5
Printed in the United States of America

85 86 87 88 89   10 9 8 7 6 5 4 3 2 1

Library of Congress Cataloging in Publication Data

Blamires, Harry.
  Words made flesh.

  1. Meditations.   I. Title.
BV4832.2.B534 1985   242   85-2162
ISBN 0-89283-235-5

Acknowledgement

To my friend Michael Spencer Ellis for his
kindness in reading through my typescript and for
his helpful comments on it.

Thanks are also due to Mr. John Blackburn for
permission to quote from Thomas Blackburn's
poem, "Hospital for Defectives," from the
collection *The Next Word* (1958) published by
Putnam, London.

CONTENTS

Introduction · 1

Fire · 5

Water · 11

Ark/Vessel · 17

Air/Breath · 23

Earth · 27

Tree · 33

Rock/Stone · 39

Blood · 45

Wine · 51

Body · 57

Bread · 63

Door and Key · 69

The Way · 75

Home · 81

House · 87

Table · 93

Milk · 99

Debt · 103

Inheritance · 109

Hands · 113

Potter and Clay · 119

Garden · 123

Face · 127

Eyes · 133

Veil · 139

Tongue/Voice · 145

Head · 151

Crown · 157

Bride · 163

Word · 169

Introduction

MY BOOK *On Christian Truth* made direct study of doctrines which explain the nature of God and his dealing with us. This book turns to consideration of things in human life and the human environment which deepen our understanding of those truths. Exploration of Christian truth naturally transforms our view of the world around us. It enables us to make sense of things we never understood before. Conversely, our growing insight into the world around us amplifies and enriches what we have learned of God directly from Christian teaching.

Things supernatural and spiritual can be explained only in terms of our own earthly experience. For this reason there has been controversy in our age about how we ought or ought not to use words in describing God. The scholar will say that human language is inadequate to describe what God is like. But human language is also inadequate to describe what a symphony by Beethoven is like. In either case a wise person will try to make himself acquainted with the real thing at first hand before attempting a description for the benefit of others. Having pondered the symphony and its effect on him in several performances, a listener might then hazard an attempt at description and say: "The music sometimes swirls like a tornado and at other times it flows like a mountain stream; in places it jolts you violently like an earthquake, and in other places it wraps itself gently around you like a soft mist." From Old Testament days people who have tried to tell others what God is like have made use of similarly colorful imagery, appealing to experience of fire and thunder, mountain and sunlight.

However, there is a crucial difference between using

1

imagery of storm or stream, fire or light, in explaining what a symphony is like and using such imagery in explaining what God is like. God himself made the storm and the stream, the fire and the light. This is the peculiarity about describing God in words. We say he is "sure as a rock" and that his wisdom is "deep as the sea"; but God himself made the rock and made the sea, and even made the brains which we use to name them in words. All things are products of his mind and hand.

When you study a maker's products—the pictures he has painted or the books he has written—you learn something about the character of the maker himself. You would expect knowledge of the life and personality of Milton to shed light on the poetry he wrote; and you would expect knowledge of the poetry to reveal the character of its creator. There is a two-way connection. The more you understand the one, the more you will understand the other. This two-way connection affects all comparisons you make between a creator and his creation. The statement "God's wisdom is deep as the sea" tells you something about the sea as well as something about God's wisdom. The Old Testament insists that the sea and the hills, the sky and the rocks bear the marks of their Maker. We need to attend to them in that respect. Anyone who wants to learn the most about a great writer or artist will have to study carefully everything that he wrote or made. The more we examine the world God has made and the kind of life he has designed for us in it, the more we shall learn of him. As the literary man is forever interrelating what he knows about an author from his personal biographical details with what he learns from his various books, so the Christian must be continually interrelating what he learns of God through religious teaching and experience with what he learns of him from the world he has made. And the more the Christian pursues these interrelationships, the more conscious he will become of the sheer coherence of the Christian faith, its universal applicability. The created world and the experience of its inhabitants, viewed within this context, turn out to be all of a piece. The poet Dryden had a phrase for the revelation that is given to us—"All, all of a piece throughout."

Then where do we start to explore this all-of-a-pieceness? We have already noted that in Christian tradition certain things in the created world have been referred to repeatedly in the effort to describe what God is like in his own nature and in his effect upon men and women. There are also things in our environment which have acquired special significance because God's incarnate Son made particular use of them or particular reference to them in his teaching. These things are still about us in our daily life. For instance, fire and sea, bread and blood, are both objects of daily experience and, in different ways, images of crucial significance in God's revelation. This book attempts to look at such things afresh in the light of what they have meant to Christians in the past and in the light of what they can still mean for us today.

It would be inadequate to say, in the usual sense of the expression, that this is a book about words. But it is certainly a book about words in the sense that the entire universe is God's utterance; that everything in it, in one way or another, tells us what God has to say. For this reason the chapters of the book culminate in a chapter on the supreme utterance of God, the incarnate Word. You understand a detective novel fully only when you reach the final chapter which pulls all the accumulated clues together by relating them to the one crucial clue, the master-clue, which sheds new light on all the rest. So in this book explorations of the meanings of individual words will be given their full relevance and significance only by relating them to the crucial Word, the Key-Word, the Master-Word who sheds new light on all other utterances of God's glory.

ONE

Fire

I WAS BROUGHT UP in northern England in an area where, even
during the privations of the interwar Depression, coal was
by today's standards comparatively cheap, and even quite poor
people managed to keep a good fire burning in their kitchen
grate. "I like to keep a good fire." As a child I heard many a
housewife, and many a poor one at that, say those words with
relish and pride. It was a point of honor. "Whatever else, I
always manage to keep a good fire." And often the speaker
would add, "I'd rather go hungry than cold." Keeping warm
had about it the air of a duty as well as a comfort. There was an
unwritten law which would have made it shameful to keep
house with no fire blazing. And when I first went to live in the
south, in Oxford, and to encounter a different breed of people,
a different social class (who had admittedly a less damp and
chilly climate to deal with), I was astonished and dismayed to
make my first contact with human beings for whom not having
a fire was regarded as virtuous rather than shameful. Being
cold seemed to give these well-heeled people the same sense of
dutifully serving some high principle as keeping warm gave
the poor old retired domestic servant or millhand in the north.
Here were people who could say, "We rarely light a fire
between April and October," and instead of hanging their
heads in shame and guilt, they looked you proudly and boldly
in the eyes for a sign of answering admiration.

My sympathies have never been with such people. A good fire in the grate was, physically and emotionally speaking, the essential center of the home in my young days. Yet the word *fire* can of course call out associations very different from those of homely cosiness. If I were awakened in the middle of the night on the ninth floor of a hotel and heard someone shouting "Fire!" I should no doubt leap out of bed in horror. Fire is one of those words that can delight or terrify; for fire itself is one of those things that can bring pleasure and comfort or agony and destruction. I understand that in Hebrew two different words were used for the verb "to burn": when incense of a sacrifice was being offered to God with a sweet-smelling savor and when a city was being destroyed by conflagration. But comforting or destructive, in English fire is fire and burning is burning. You may "burn" with the love of God. (*Incendium Amoris*, "the fire of love," is the title of a religious treatise by the fourteenth-century hermit and mystic, Richard Rolle of Hampole.) You may "burn" with the fire of lust—and St. Paul says it is better to marry. God destroyed Sodom and Gomorrah with fire from heaven. Cloven tongues of fire descended upon the apostles' heads at Pentecost.

There is a celebrated hymn to the Holy Spirit by Charles Wesley:

> O thou who camest from above
> The fire celestial to impart,
> Kindle a flame of sacred love
> On the mean altar of my heart.
> There let it for thy glory burn
> With inextinguishable blaze
> And trembling to its source return
> In humble prayer and fervent praise.

The idea of the fire in the heart here is that it blazes like a fire on an altar. The implication is that what is being offered up in sacrifice is indeed the self and self-centeredness. Even an "inextinguishable blaze" can be a good thing in some contexts. Indeed superficially "destructive" connotations of the word *fire* in the Bible often have a positive aspect. The obliteration of Sodom and Gomorrah cannot be called "destructive" in any but the most superficial sense, since it is always constructive to get rid of human wickedness. We have to remember not only that fire gives heat and that fire consumes but also that it cleanses. God is "like a refiner's fire and like a fuller's soap," Malachi tells us (Mal 3:2). The two images match interestingly. They refer to cleansing operations in two different trades: that of one who separates the precious metal from the dross and that of one who beats and treads the dirt out of cloth. Malachi develops the first parallel. "He shall purify the sons of Levi and purge them as gold and silver, that they may offer unto the Lord an offering in righteousness" (Mal 3:3). Reading such words, one begins to wonder where the extraordinary idea came from that Christians have traditionally pictured God as a venerable old man with a white beard seated in majesty. They have rather pictured him doing a full-time job in the refinery or the mill. They have likened him to a boilerman stoking up a furnace or to a workman treading the dirt out of cloth.

These likenesses are not one-sided; they are reciprocal. A mistake many Christians (especially "theologians") have made in recent years is to think that in describing God as being, say, like a father, or a king, or a shepherd, we are dealing with connections that are fanciful—helpful perhaps, but essentially fanciful. They are not. They are connections which tell us a lot about fathers, kings, and shepherds, as well as a lot about God. It is not just that, having first learned that God is our father, we should then picture God differently: we should change our concept of fatherhood too. Indeed we begin to glimpse why God invented earthly fatherhood, what it is all about in the whole scheme of things. Similarly, if God's activity can be described as being like the stoker's or the fuller's, that is not just a picturesque portrayal of God; it also guarantees the divine element in the labor of the man who controls your heating or manufactures your new suit.

My starting point took us back to the days when most households in my country had an open fire. Some of my readers might well have nodded their heads and muttered to themselves, "Here is a fellow with his thoughts in the past. It was all right fifty years ago talking about God's love in human life in terms of a fire in the living-room hearth; but that's all gone. These days we just flick a switch and turn the knob of the thermostat."

But surely, surely, in terms of the way God works among us, a central heating system is even more expressive of some aspects of his care than a coal fire or a log fire. With an open fire you're always having to leave your chair to shovel some more coal on or to poke a log aside. And if you fall asleep in your chair, the fire will die into ash. The central heating system, however, works invisibly, unobtrusively, protecting your environment by means of a concealed and, roughly speaking, never-failing source of heat. That is how, physically and spiritually, life is made livable. And that is how God looks after us.

We tend to think of life as presenting us with "good" things and "bad" things, "nice" things and "unpleasant" things: steaks and sunsets and symphonies and lilies on the one hand; rats and cancers and volcanoes and earthquakes on the other hand. But the most basic and the best things in life cannot be thus classified. Fire is an instance. It is the most comforting thing in the world when you are feeling cold. It is the most painful thing in the world when you are thrown into it. It is the source of energy, light, and warmth, and yet it can terrify, scorch, and torment. God makes his ministers "a flame of fire" (Heb 1:7) and his Holy Spirit alighted in flame on the heads of the apostles. But when the Son of Man shall come in glory and before him shall be gathered all nations, and he shall separate them one from another as a shepherd divides his sheep from the goats, the sheep on the right and the goats on the left, what will he say to those on the left? "Depart from me, ye cursed, into everlasting fire, prepared for the devil and his angels" (Mt 25:41).

There is an old classical story of how the centaur Nessus carried Deianira across a river and then tried to rape her. Deianira was the wife of Hercules, and he killed Nessus with a poisoned arrow. When dying, Nessus gave some of his blood to Deianira. It had the power to arouse love, he assured her. And long afterwards, when Hercules was unfaithful to Deianira, she tried to win him back by sending him a shirt soaked in this potent blood. But Nessus had tricked her, for when Hercules put the shirt on it burned him and, desperate with the unbearable pain of it, Hercules threw himself on a funeral pyre and destroyed himself by fire. To escape one kind of burning, he chose another kind of burning. To escape the agony of his garment, he chose the agony of self-immolation.

In his poem *Four Quartets,* T.S. Eliot draws some interesting parallels from this story. The shirt was sent by Deianira out of love for Hercules and out of desire to regain his love. The pain it inflicted on him compelled him to choose between the torment of wearing an irremovable garment and the torment of self-sacrifice on a pyre. The latter is chosen because it is final. Eliot indicates that in a sense God has given us "a shirt of flame" in the form of the passions and appetites natural to men and women who are clothed in human flesh. We can writhe in the intolerable torment of it, or we can fling ourselves on the pyre of self-sacrifice. We can burn with unsatisfied desire, or we can throw ourselves into the fire of God's love. In short, the fire of God's love which cleanses is the only alternative to the fire of hell which endlessly torments.

> We only live, only suspire
> Consumed by either fire or fire.

Eliot suggests other aspects of the same paradox. He recalls the way Dido, queen of Carthage, destroyed herself in despair after her lover Aeneas forsook her and sailed away to Rome. She killed herself and was cremated on a great funeral pyre. This is one kind of destruction by love and by fire. Another kind of destruction by love and by fire is that which martyred Christians endured at the stake.

The only hope, or else despair
Lies in the choice of pyre or pyre—
To be redeemed from fire by fire.

That is the Christian's vocation. To be redeemed from the fire of passion and appetite, frustration and despair, by the fire of the cleansing, self-immolating love of God.

TWO

Water

WE THINK OF WATER as the thing that can save us from destruction by fire. If our house catches fire we call for the fire brigade, and their fire engine, as well as being a vehicle for getting them quickly to the scene of the fire, is a machine equipped to draw water from the main and to direct it in forceful jets onto the flames. But water is a blessing in far more ways than this. It is a basic necessity of human life.

Most of us have at some time or another burned ourselves, if only on the fingers by picking up a plate that is too hot to hold. And we have all at some time or other been cold and felt a desperate need for the warmth that fire brings. But how many of us who have personally tasted how agonizing death by fire must be have also tasted how overwhelming death by water must be? And how many of us who have shivered in longing for fire have personally panted with parched throat and lips for a drink of water? There is no doubt that in Middle Eastern countries and other regions of the world where people have firsthand experience of blazing sunshine beating down on parched deserts, consciousness of the blessings of water must be sharper and more sensitive than in countries where rainfall is more likely to seem too lavish than too sparse. "My soul thirsteth for thee," the psalmist cries to God, "my flesh longeth for thee in a dry and thirsty land where no water is" (Ps 63:1). It is not easy for an Englishman to enter feelingly into such pleas. I saw a display in a charity shop window last week. Some imaginative person had tried to convey to the inhabitants of this damp island of ours exactly what lack of water can mean in poverty-stricken areas of the third world. The window was littered with bare stones. An empty vessel and a skeleton-like human figure drove the message home.

No wonder the imagery of the Bible is rich in references to the watering of the earth. The Israelites were narrowly saved from dying of thirst in the desert. Moses struck a rock and life-giving water flowed from it to revive and refresh them. Parallels have often been drawn between this fountain of restoration and the flow of water and blood which came from Christ's side on the cross. For Christ is the rock, and his side was pierced by a sword as the rock in the wilderness had been struck. Many a hymn speaks of the water and the blood from Christ's side as a life-giving stream.

> Rock of ages, cleft for me,
> Let me hide myself in thee;
> Let the water and the blood,
> From thy riven side which flowed,
> Be of sin the double cure:
> Cleanse me from its guilt and power.

This cleansing, life-restoring power of water is represented in its use in baptism. We think of Jesus as a well of living water, for when he spoke with the woman of Samaria who met him at the wellhead, he so described himself. Whoever drinks of this well's water will thirst again, but not so the person who drinks of the water I shall give him, "a well of water springing up into everlasting life" (Jn 4:14).

In the Western world we don't, most of us, draw water from wells anymore. We turn a tap. But the water answers the same daily needs of drinking and washing. Somehow it seems to smack of disrespect to compare Jesus to a waterworks engineer and to describe his gift to us as a tap. But if we are indeed in a world in which God has made the water of life everywhere available to us, then he seems to have constructed something very like a modern water storage and distribution system. If the reservoirs of his saving love are inexhaustible, if the channels of his grace flow everywhere, not obvious to the naked eye but hidden under all the business and paraphernalia of modern life, then indeed it all sounds very much like the way water finds its way through underground pipes to our kitchen sink. If so, we have to learn to turn a tap when we are spiritually parched as well as when we are physically thirsty; we have to turn on the shower when we are sticky with sin as well as when we are sticky with sweat.

Indeed the message of Christ is that we are not isolated in spiritual deserts. We do not all live in lonely oases. We are all connected by a network of pipes to the reservoirs of God's grace. We can choose to turn on the tap or not to turn it. We are all on the main. That is exactly what Christendom is, that part of the world which is on the spiritual main. The pre-Christian world may have had its rivers and lakes, its fountains and wells. But it was the Christian church which constructed the great dams that gathered the waters of divine grace in massive reservoirs and channeled them this way and that way across the world wherever the word was taken. Of course we can if we wish disconnect ourselves from the system through which the waters of life flow by turning off the main shutoff valve. That is what we do if we leave the church.

It is odd that I should be writing today about saving grace in terms of flowing water, for we have just had one of the wettest weeks in my memory. The roads have been awash. The lakes hereabouts have overflowed their banks and so have the rivers. There are flooded fields everywhere. Water, like fire, can damage. Indeed, when God all but destroyed humanity for its wickedness it was not fire that he used but flood. We shall examine the image of the ark in the next chapter. Meanwhile let us not forget that the dual power of water to cleanse or swamp, to revive or to drown, is as much an aspect of Christian imagery as is the dual power of fire. Such paradoxes are built into the human situation. Life is never simplistic; neither is our world. The sea in which we bathe delightedly on golden beaches under the summer sun is the same sea whose tidal wave leaves acres of farmland waterlogged, homes wrecked, and corpses bloated like sponges. No wonder the Bible is rich in imagery of the destructive power of water as well as of its life-giving power. The psalmist describes the massive military defeat his people have been rescued from in terms of water swallowing them up. That is what God has saved them from. Without him "the waters had overwhelmed us, the stream had gone over our soul: the proud waters had gone over our soul" (Ps 124:4-5). The Song of Solomon's greatest protestation of the power of love is that "many waters cannot quench love, neither can the floods drown it" (Sg 8:7). Water, like fire, can be man's enemy as well as his friend. When the psalmist wants to stress the past trials and tribulations of the Israelites he says, "We went through fire and through water" (Ps 66:12), and the expression is still used to describe a nerve-wracking experience that tests one to the uttermost.

The human mind adapts itself readily to the gymnastic flexibility of words. If a man tells you that he has been through fire and water, you know that fire and water are above all things to be escaped from. If a man tells you that he was wrecked on a desert island without fire or water, you know that fire and water are above all things to be desired. Christian baptism reflects this duality in the power of water to refresh or to overwhelm. We must not sentimentalize baptism as simply an experience of being refreshed by the life-giving waters of grace, for that is only half the story of baptism. The Christian's baptism is also a death by water—death to sin and to worldliness. The old Adam is drowned that the new man may live in Christ.

The skies shower down rain on the parching earth. The skies showered down loathsome plagues on the recalcitrant Egyptians. The word *rain* is freely used for the downpour that nourishes the earth or for the downpour of shells that blackens and craters it. When Edith Sitwell wrote a poem about her experience of German air raids on London in 1940, she likened the incendiary downpour—the terrible price of human wickedness—with the rain of blood from Christ's cross. The noise of bombs dropping around is like the hammering of nails into the cross or the tramping of feet on Christ's tomb. As raid follows raid, night and morning, the poet reminds us that each day and each night our sins nail Christ afresh to his cross.

> Still falls the Rain
> At the feet of the Starved Man hung upon the Cross.
> Christ that each day, each night, nails there,
>   have mercy on us . . .

THREE

Ark/Vessel

C HRIST WALKED UPON THE WATER. He stilled the storm. Turbulent seas have always provided imagery of life's storm and stress.

> O Lord, the pilot's part perform,
> And guide and guard me through the storm;
> Defend me from each threatening ill,
> Control the waves, say, "Peace, be still."

In such words the poet William Cowper prayed for strength and guidance in temptation. Many a hymn speaks of life's progress as a voyage across a stormy sea. We are tempest-tossed in being subject to the daily trials and tribulations of human life.

Not many of us think naturally nowadays of voyaging across the sea. We have got used to journeying by air. But when I first visited the United States in 1961 I sailed from Southampton to New York on the *Queen Mary* and back again a month later in the old *Queen Elizabeth*. The outward journey was made in early March. The crossing was a turbulent one. For two days we had the hatches battened down and were not allowed to go on deck. For two days scarcely anyone came down to breakfast or any other meal. The fortunate few could eat as much as they wanted. The stewards were only too happy to ply us with helping after helping: roasts and steaks, strawberries and cream, whatever one wanted. For two days the floors beneath us rose and fell, things slithered across tables and down sloping floors, and we grasped at rails as we lurched unsteadily from dining room to cabin.

Yet we did not feel that at any moment the waves might overwhelm us and the sea swallow us up. Indeed, I have just read an advertisement for Cunard cruises which draws attention to the great days of transatlantic voyages in these words: "In August 1938 an awesome quarter mile of palatial grand hotel crossed the Atlantic from New York at 30 knots." I do not imagine that William Cowper had in mind a mobile quarter mile of hotel when he called upon God to pilot him safely through the storms of temptation. Voyaging across stormy seas once meant facing the possibility of being swallowed up. When John Donne set sail for Germany in 1619 he wrote a poem of prayer, committing himself to God:

> In what torn ship soever I embark,
> That ship shall be my emblem of thy Ark;
> What sea soever swallow me, that flood
> Shall be to me an emblem of thy blood . . .

He insists on regarding the ship in which he voyages as the ark in which God saved Noah from drowning. But he refuses to look upon the seas as hostile. If they swallow him up, let it be like being submerged in the flood of Christ's redeeming blood. This of course is a traditional image. William Cowper wrote:

> There is a fountain filled with blood
>   Drawn from Emmanuel's veins;
> And sinners, plunged beneath that flood,
>   Lose all their guilty stains.

It is characteristic of Donne to run together the image of his ship as the ark of salvation and the image of the ocean as the flood of Christ's redeeming blood. And he develops the second image in a novel way:

> I sacrifice this island unto thee,
> And all whom I loved there, and who loved me;
> When I have put our seas twixt them and me,
> Put thou thy sea betwixt my sins and thee.

Thus his prayer continues. In leaving his family and his homeland and putting the sea between them and himself, he is making a sacrifice to Christ. He prays that in return Christ will put *his* sea (the sea of his redeeming blood) between Donne's sins and himself. No doubt Donne's image of thrusting his sins to a distance was influenced by the psalmist's words, "As far as the east is from the west, so far hath he removed our transgressions from us" (Ps 103:12).

We may well wonder whether, like John Donne, but over 350 years later, when setting out on a journey, we can commit ourselves to God's keeping with similar imagery:

> In what jet plane soever I embark,
> That plane shall be my emblem of thy Ark.

It may not sound quite right. Yet every journey taken is a miniature of the progress through life. Each journey ought to remind us that we are always in God's hands. For the dangers of a journey but intensify the ordinary dangers of daily life. We may be especially conscious, when we are sitting in a jumbo jet poised above the clouds in mid-Atlantic, that life is precarious and that a little human miscalculation or mechanical failure or indeed an "act of God" could bring sudden disaster and death. But in fact we are even more at risk, statistically speaking, when we drive along a highway; more still perhaps when we walk where there is motor traffic. I do not know who the wit was who observed that since far more people die in their beds than are killed on the roads, it is safer to take a drive than to go to bed at night; but he was justly aware of how we are daily and nightly at risk. We ought not to have to wait until we are making a long journey before we entrust ourselves consciously into God's hands.

Noah's ark was the vessel in which he and his family, and through them the human race, were saved from the flood. It was natural that the ark in which mankind had been rescued should have been regarded for all time as a vessel of salvation. Hence the Church came to be regarded as our ark of salvation. When Donne, therefore, saw his ship as an "emblem" of God's "ark" he was, like Cowper, thinking in terms of a long-standing connection between the pilgrimage of life and a voyage under God's protection and pilotage. But *ark* (like vessel) has been used of containers much smaller than ships. In particular it was used of the sacred wooden chest carried through the desert by the Israelites and containing the two tablets on which the Ten Commandments were inscribed. We must remember that, in Noah's case, when the waters of the flood subsided, God gave him a solemn pledge ("made a covenant" with him, as the Bible puts it) that he would never again destroy all life by a flood, and the rainbow appeared in the sky as the sign of this pledge. The portable ark of the Israelites, in containing the tablets of the commandments, was once again the symbol of a compact between God and his people.

The word "vessel" has also been applied to people as being "containers." In Ananias' dream the Lord said of St. Paul, "He is a chosen vessel unto me, to bear my name before the Gentiles" (Acts 9:15). This usage was applied in later days to the Virgin Mary in whose body the divine Savior was carried before birth. Sometimes, more specifically, it was applied to the Virgin's womb as the container of the divine being. Here was another extension of the expression "ark of salvation."

Not surprisingly, therefore, the word "Ark" was eventually used poetically of the Virgin Mary as the vessel through whom a new covenant was established between God and man, and in whose body humanity was renewed and the race saved. It was a small step from this to seeing a symbolic connection between the womb as the vessel in which God was made flesh and the chalice as the vessel in which Christ's blood was made available to his people. The womblike shape of the chalice encouraged the drawing of this parallel.

We have come a long way from the image of the ship conveying its passengers, the Ark containing Noah, the chest containing the old covenant, to the womb containing the new one, and to the chalice holding the sacramental blood. The little knot of images is one that can be fruitfully pondered. All Christian moral teaching revolves around making relationships between ourselves and Christ and seeing his earthly ways as the pattern of our own ways. This is what we have been taught to do—to build our lives in him. The kinship of universal brotherhood and sisterhood in Christ is what we are asked to claim. This being so, we have the duty as well as the right to draw parallels between his course on earth and ours. We are always being told that we must each be ready to bear our cross. If that is what we learn from the end of his life, what do we learn from the beginning? The ark of Noah, which preserved humanity from a new beginning, was a vessel in which life was secure. The womb of Mary, which preserved humanity for a new beginning, was a vessel in which life was secure. The protecting and keeping secure of whatever is entrusted to our keeping is one of the most elementary obligations of humanity. How can a man or a woman decide to make the vessel containing a new life a condemned cell, a vehicle carrying its occupant to the guillotine, a poisoned chalice? That is what abortion does.

FOUR

Air/Breath

W E TRAVEL NOW BY AIR rather than by sea. And movement through air is very different from movement through water. There is such a thing as atmospheric turbulence that can render a flight less than smooth. The pilot warns us to fasten our seat belts when the plane seems to be approaching a pocket of such turbulence. But it is very different from a storm at sea—very different from watching the waves tower above the decks, feeling the ground beneath us rise and fall at every taking of breath, lurching with walls and staircases from side to side, struggling like a baby of two to guide a cup vertically and horizontally from table to mouth. A few minutes in the grip of a seat belt and the odd jolt as though we were driving a car over a rough track are scarcely to be compared with the battened-down hatches and the "quarter mile of palatial grand hotel" lurching and slithering as though there were a never-ending earthquake.

Water is a tenuous substance, but at least you can gather two handfuls of it and throw it over your face. By comparison with air it is graspable, tangible, measurable. What makes movement through air so different from movement through water is the insubstantiality of air. When we go for a swim or take a shower we find water palpable. In the sea we can lash at it, beat it, swirl it around. If we try to make a comparable impression on the air, we fail. A popular expression for human activity that

23

is totally ineffectual and pointless is to say, "It was like beating the air." Air is impalpable; air is invisible; yet for human survival from one moment to the next air is the most essential commodity of all. We can last a day or two without water. We cannot survive five minutes without air. Breathing is more basic than eating or drinking.

Small wonder then that when primitive man wanted a word to define the divine impulse which animates all things and which sustains a human being invisibly and impalpably he should have chosen the word *breath* or *spirit* (which is Latin for "breath"). And we can scarcely today begin to understand what the working of the Holy Spirit is like unless we recall how at every moment breath is taken in and let out, for the most part effortlessly and unconsciously. Inhaling and exhaling, we go about our business. And unless we happen to be victims of asthma or bronchitis, emphysema or heart trouble, we take our breathing for granted. Ironically enough we take most for granted what we could least do without. I was reminded of this last week by an aging friend with a sense of humor. I met him in the street and said, "You have to be thankful if you can still enjoy your food and walk about." He corrected me slyly. "If you can still breathe," he murmured.

Spirit is breath. The air goes in and out of our lungs. On a small scale it is like the way a coal mine is ventilated. An engine keeps the fans turning that move air through every hidden underground corridor. For that matter it is like the way a subway is ventilated. This permeation of the entire inner network by the unfailing invisible movement of breath is like the permeation of our inner beings by the movement of the Spirit.

Spirit therefore is not a colorless word nor even a vague concept. It may suggest the impalpable and the invisible, but it cannot suggest anything less than something that is crucial and in effect solid and vital. For without ventilation all life and movement within the mine falters and falls. Without ventilation passengers and employees in the subway wilt and collapse.

Thus ventilation is known by its effects. The movement of air outside is known by the turning of the windmill sails, by the fluttering of the flag, by the sweeping back of the hair. The movement of air underground is known by the continuing drilling at the working face, by the walking passengers who board the train. The movement of air within us is known by the skating of hand across paper to pen this line. "Ah yes, the wind is still blowing. It must be. Look at the swaying branches of the tree." "Ah yes, breathing is still continuing. . . . It must be. For see, he is lifting his hand to his face and adjusting his spectacles." The spirit is at work too, though you can no more point to him than you can point to the wind that sways the tree and to the breath which makes possible the raising of the arm.

There are circumstances in which we rely on air conditioning systems. I do not just mean the air conditioning which ensure that we shall be kept cool indoors when the temperature is high outside. For this is a safeguard of comfort as much as of health. I mean the air conditioning in the aircraft which ensures that we can breathe naturally and remain conscious and alert. In a sense the church's practices and disciplines are a kind of spiritual air-conditioning system. By worship, by prayer, by Bible-reading, by the sacraments, we maintain a conditioning of the spiritual atmosphere that guarantees our continuing life in the Spirit even in an environment where secularism has reduced the level of oxygen so drastically that people are flopping down all around us in spiritual debility and moribundity. The cost of this is mental sickness is appalling "The air pressure is failing. Will passengers kindly put on their oxygen masks"—that is too often the situation of Christians in today's spiritual atmosphere.

What can you do with air? You can blow it into a balloon with such a pressure that the balloon floats away in the sky. You can blow it inside soapy water in such a way that a filmy skin encloses your breath and carries it floating away on the wind. If you know how to do it, you can blow air into a clarinet or a French horn and a pleasing sound comes out. Your breath goes in and is transformed into a noise: nothing very remarkable about that. After all the breath that comes from our lungs is forever being transformed into noise when we speak. As we wrapped the filmy skin around our breath to form a bubble, so we can blow out vowels and wrap consonants around them to make words. This is one of the most exciting things about spoken words. They are air that has been knocked into shape; breath that has been piped into vowels and then parceled up within consonants into syllables and words. Sir John Davies, a poet of the Elizabethan age, wrote a delightful poem called *Orchestra* in which he saw all life in terms of a dance. There is the dance of the stars in heaven. There is the tidal dance of the sea around earth's shores. There is the dance of the water from sea to sky, from cloud to earth, from stream to sea. There is the dance of the succeeding seasons. There is the dance of human life from cradle to grave. And there is the dance of the air in sounds and words.

> For what are breath, speech, echoes, music, winds
> But dancings of the Air, in sundry kinds?

The image is an interesting one. It is by the pressure of air and the molding of it that a word takes shape. The relationship of breath to word is subtle but binding and inextricable. So is the relationship of the Holy Spirit to the divine Word. "And when he had said this, he breathed on them, and saith unto them, 'Receive ye the Holy Ghost'" (Jn 20:22).

The Old Testament tells how "the Lord God formed man of the dust of the ground, and breathed into his nostrils the breath of life; and man became a living soul" (Gn 2:7). And the New Testament tells us, "And when Jesus had cried with a loud voice, he said, Father into thy hands I commend my spirit: and having said thus, he gave up the ghost" (Lk 23:46). John Donne, in one of his finest sermons, drew a connection between these two events. "As God breathed a soul into the first Adam, so this second Adam breathed his soul into God, into the hands of God."

FIVE

Earth

THE AIR SUSTAINS US, but it is of the earth that we are made. It is by eating the fruits of the earth that our bodies grow: or it is by eating the bodies of the animals that have themselves fed on the fruits of the earth. As creatures of flesh and blood we derive our substance from the earth—and when we die our bodies are restored to the earth, the earth from which the nourishment of new generations will be drawn in grain and vegetables, fruit and meat. This cyclic process by which grain becomes bread, then human flesh, then a corpse, then manure to nourish new grain, is enacted in miniature day by day as we eat food from the earth and excrete the waste back to earth. There is a comic Yorkshire dialect song well-known in England, "On Ilkla Moor baht'at" ("On Ilkley Moor without hat"). Translated, it runs thus, verse by verse:

"Where have you been since I saw you?"
On Ilkley Moor without hat
"I've been a-courting Mary Jane"
On Ilkley Moor without hat
"You're going to get your death of cold"
On Ilkley Moor . . . (repeated after every line)
"Then we shall have to bury you"
"Then worms will come and eat you up"
"Then ducks will come and eat the worms"

"Then we shall come and eat the ducks"
"Then we shall all have eaten you"

The Bible traces the cycle too. "In the sweat of thy face shalt thou eat bread, till thou return unto the ground; for out of it thou wast taken; for dust thou art, and unto dust shalt thou return" (Gn 3:19).

In our Lord's parable of the sower, we are the earth. The seed which is the word of God is sown in us. According to the quality of our soil, the seed will take root and flourish or wither away. God's evangelists, it appears, are farmers. We are their fields. They sow the word. Sometimes God seems to go in for intensive farming: compulsive preaching comes a person's way and he is rapidly converted, at least for a time. Sometimes God's call to men and women is backed up by some accident or calamity, some injury or bereavement, that rocks them out of complacency and compels them to think deeply about the meaning of life and death. These strokes of bad fortune that suddenly come our way and turn our thoughts again to God are rather like chemical additives which act as stimulants to our otherwise unresponsive soil. Sometimes it is rather experiences of great joy which call out gratitude in us and renew our efforts in God's service. I suppose we can regard such blessings as divine subsidies to aid the cereal productiveness of our souls. Certainly the relevance of the parable of the sower has not been lost with the coming of modern agricultural techniques.

We men and women are of the earth, earthy. In Shakespeare's *Julius Caesar,* Mark Antony looks down at the stabbed corpse of Caesar and exclaims, "O pardon me, thou bleeding piece of earth!" We are all pieces of earth. Yet we are assured by the psalmist and by St. Paul that "the earth is the Lord's, and the fulness thereof" (Ps 24:1; 1 Cor 10:26). Moreover God himself became a "creature" of earth. This is one of the most distinctive truths of Christianity. "God became man," we say, and we visualize Jesus Christ as he is portrayed by artists in pictures and on walls and in stained-glass windows. He is a sweet little baby or a fresh-faced boy or a well-groomed, long-robed young man. But God becoming man meant something more than becoming a being with bright eyes and lustrous hair, with a sturdy walk, fine features, and a sensitive hand. It also meant becoming a being who chewed, masticated, and digested. A being who consumed chopped-up pieces of meat from slaughtered animals, eggs from a hencoop, and bread from grain grown in the soil. Sometimes he had to pick his teeth and blow his nose, cut his toenails, and scratch his back. As much as you and I he was involved in that cycle from corpse to worm to duck, to living, eating man and woman. Air and fire are the least tangible elements, and these are the elements of the Holy Spirit. Earth is the crudest, solidest element, and this is the element of the incarnate Son of God.

Yet if the earth is the crudest of the elements, it is also the most fruitful. The Bible has a lot to say about the fruits of the earth. The cycle of fruitfulness is common to the earth and to the animal and the human worlds. The earth is plowed up, the seed is sown, hidden away, buried in the soil, and the new life develops, first unseen, then slowly emerging above ground, in due course to ripen and be harvested. An ancient tradition in human thinking has naturally linked this process closely with the process of human reproduction. The physical similarity between plowing the earth to plant the seed and impregnating a woman is such that in vulgar language words for the two processes have sometimes in the past been interchangeable. In Shakespeare's *Antony and Cleopatra,* Agrippa praises the charm and beauty of Cleopatra and says how she lured even Julius Caesar to be her lover and to beget a son on her. This is how he puts it:

She made great Caesar lay his sword to bed,
He ploughed her and she cropped.

An interesting thing about these lines is that alongside the notion of plowing the sword introduces the notion of wounding. In Shakespeare's day words such as *sword* and *weapon* had the same sexual connotations as words from husbandry such as *dibble*. Impregnating a woman is naturally seen in terms of pushing the seed into the earth: it is also seen in terms of wounding. The earth is wounded by the plow and by the dibble.

The notion of wounding is important in this context because it is closely related to the idea of death. The earth dies in winter to be reborn in spring. Or one may say, the seed is buried only to bring forth new life. An old tradition of our language uses the word *dying* of a woman's physical surrender at the climax which brings conception. She "dies" in that she submits to being "wounded" by man, and thus becomes the source of new life. The English poet Elizabeth Jennings wrote a poem, "Song for a Birth or a Death," in which she toys with the theme that "all matings mean a kill":

> And human creatures kissed in trust
> Feel the blood throb to death until
> The seed is struck, the pleasures done . . .

The cycle of the seasons from death to birth matches this human cycle from "death" to birth. In each case the seed is planted, hidden, and slowly bursts into growth.

But Christ too is wounded, dies, is buried in the tomb, and is reborn on Easter day. This sequence of events repeats archetypally the pattern which the life of earth follows from year to year and the life of humanity from generation to generation.

We are told that as Christians we must lose ourselves in Christ, that his way has to be our way. And parallels can be drawn between the way in which new life is engendered in Mother Earth or in a human mother and the way new spiritual life is born in any man or woman. For we all have to learn to submit ourselves to the wounding invasion of our personality by the Holy Spirit, as the earth is wounded by the plow and a woman by the invading male. We have to "die" in the wintry act of self-commitment. The seed of the Spirit is buried within us as the seed is buried in the earth. Christ gave us the parable of the sower to remind us that the seed may be fruitless if the ground is stony or thick with thorns. For us who are children of the old Adam, being reborn into the new humanity made available in Christ has parallels with the pattern of reproduction in the life of earth and of the human family.

The "wounding" of a woman in procreation is a wounding effected in love. The "wounding" of the earth in plowing is wounding that is not meant to damage but to bring forth fruit. The wounding of our pride and self-centeredness which God's demand effects is also bred of his love for us and of his desire that we should bring forth fruit. The wounding that is meant to injure or destroy is a very different matter altogether. It is bred of hatred and self-centeredness. When Eve plucks the apple from the forbidden tree in Milton's *Paradise Lost,* we are told that "Earth felt the wound." The rifling of the tree made a wound that had to be paid for by other wounds endured upon a very different tree, Christ's cross.

SIX

Tree

THE TREE IS A CENTRAL SYMBOL in Christian teaching. The forbidden tree in the Garden of Eden bore the fruit which Adam and Eve willfully ate in defiance of God's command. And Jesus was hanged upon a "tree" as a long-term consequence. St. Peter put it exactly like that when he was called before the High Priest. "The God of our Fathers has raised Jesus whom ye slew and hanged on a tree" (Acts 5:30).

There is a good deal in the Bible about the connection between the tree and its fruit. The tree is known by its fruit (Mt 7:16). A good tree brings forth good fruit and a corrupt tree corrupt fruit (Mt 7:17). St. Peter speaks of Christ as the one "who in his own self bore our sins in his own body on the tree" (1 Pt 2:24), and St. John in the book of Revelation quotes the Spirit thus: "To him that overcometh will I give to eat of the tree of life, which is in the midst of the paradise of God" (Rev 2:7). Christ, of course, may be regarded as the fruit of the tree of life. Paradoxically the tree of life may be regarded as the tree of death, the cross. When the angel Gabriel appeared to the Virgin Mary to announce that she was to be the mother of Jesus, he said, "Hail, thou that art highly favoured, the Lord is with thee; blessed art thou among women" (Lk 1:28). And when Mary went to see her cousin Elizabeth she was greeted thus: "Blessed art thou among women, and blessed is the fruit of thy womb" (Lk 1:42). The fruit of the Virgin's womb is to

be the fruit of the tree of life of which saved mankind is given
to eat.

This is one of those cases of interconnection between image
and image that strain the imagination almost too far when they
are traced. Yet the connections have always fascinated
thoughtful Christians, even when they have been pressed
beyond the point justifiable by historical fact. For instance, the
idea was toyed with that the cross of Christ was planted on the
same spot where the forbidden tree stood in the Garden of
Eden. The fancy is useful if only that it reminds us of the very
cogent connections between the two. John Donne took up the
fancy and drew very moving thoughts from it when he wrote a
hymn to God from his sickbed.

> We think that Paradise and Calvary,
> Christ's cross and Adam's tree stood in one place;
> Look, Lord, and find both Adams met in me;
> As the first Adam's sweat surrounds my face,
> May the last Adam's blood my soul embrace.

Donne felt that the sweat of his sickness on his face was the
mark of his mortality, his subjection to the weaknesses of the
flesh, his destiny to die. For so God spoke to Adam after the
Fall. "In the sweat of thy face shalt thou eat bread, till thou
return unto the ground; for out of it you wast taken: for dust
thou art, and unto dust shalt thou return" (Gn 3:19). Donne
clearly recalled the connection between the sweat on the face
of the first Adam who was condemned to toil and death, and
the sweat on the face of the second Adam who was condemned
to suffering and death in consequence. Luke tells us how in his
agony in the Garden of Gethsemane Christ's "sweat was as it
were great drops of blood falling down to the ground" (Lk
22:44). Donne's prayer is that while the sweat of sickness and
mortality pours round his face, the redeeming blood of Christ
may pour round his soul.

In the medieval period the cross, or the "tree," was

venerated in worship and hymns were written in its praise. A notable one was the famous *Vexilla Regis prodeunt* ("The banners of the King go forward") by Venantius Fortunatus who lived in the sixth century and became bishop of Poitiers.

Fulfilled is now what David told
In true prophetic song of old,
How God the heathen's King should be;
For God is reigning from the Tree.
O Tree of glory, Tree most fair,
Ordained those holy limbs to bear;
How bright in purple robes it stood,
The purple of a Savior's blood.

Though the image of Christ reigning from the tree is biblically based in that both St. Peter and St. Paul spoke of the crucifixion as a hanging upon a tree, Christ used instead an image which likened himself to a vine. "I am the true vine" (Jn 15:1), he said and later, "I am the vine, ye are the branches."

The image of the vine is notable because it is from the vine that wine derives, and Christ was to give the apostles wine to drink as representative of his own blood. This connection we must explore further later in the book. Meanwhile we note that when the book of Revelation speaks of our privilege to "eat of the tree of life," it seems to round off the story that began with Eve's eating of the forbidden tree. Eating of the fruit of that tree "brought death into the world and all our woe," as Milton puts it. But to partake of Christ's own body and blood is to consume very different fruit, the fruit that hung from the tree of Calvary, the fruit of the tree of life.

The normal picture we have of stealing fruit from a forbidden tree is that of the little boy who sneaks over into a garden or orchard, then climbs a tree and snatches an apple. George Herbert, the seventeenth-century English parish priest and poet, wrote a poem called "The Sacrifice" in which the speaker is Christ himself, speaking, as it were, from the cross and calling all who pass by to witness his suffering. Each verse of the poem has the refrain, "Was ever grief like Mine?" One daring stanza runs:

> O, all ye who pass by, behold and see
> 'Man stole the fruit, but I must climb the tree,
> The tree of life to all but only Me:
>   Was ever grief like Mine?

The cross is the tree of death to Christ and the tree of life to all others. Man had the pleasure of eating the fruit, but Christ has had to climb the tree as a result, reversing the usual sequence.

It is characteristic of the wisdom of John Milton that when Eve has just eaten of the forbidden fruit in the Garden of Eden, she breaks out in praise, indeed in worship, of the tree itself. And her words are a kind of parody of the words of veneration found in the old hymns to the cross such as the one I quoted:

> O Sovereign, virtuous, precious of all Trees
> In paradise,

she says, vowing in future to tend the tree each morning with daily praise. And as she turns from the tree to go back to Adam, she first genuflects before it. T.S. Eliot spoke of our choice of being consumed by either fire or fire, the fire of desire or the fire of the Spirit. Milton makes clear that we have the choice of worshiping tree or tree, going down on our knees before the tree of nature or the tree of life.

There was a notion in the later Middle Ages that just as the world was "whirled" round and round (puns were fashionable) so the stars of heaven danced in circuit, swinging around the axle-tree of heaven. The axle-tree became a symbol of the pivot of the revolving universe. As such the image of the axle-tree, applied to Christ's cross, has represented the cross as the axle on which the whole of our history on earth revolves. It might be scarcely worthwhile to mention this fanciful and seemingly archaic piece of symbolism. But it has been given a new lease of life in two of the most celebrated English poems of our century, T.S. Eliot's *Four Quartets* and David Jones' *Anathemata*. The latter, a very difficult poem, is rich in symbolism. It ends with images of Christ in his two self-giving postures—"recumbent" at the Last Supper and "riding the Axile Tree." The image places Christ's suffering on the cross at the center on which the whole of our human history is pivoted.

SEVEN

Rock/Stone

T HE LORD IS MY ROCK, and my fortress, and my deliverer," says the psalmist, "my strength in whom I will trust" (Ps 18:2). God is often compared to a rock in the Old Testament in order, as here, to emphasize his reliability and trustworthiness, the defense he provides against enemies and troubles. We may well wonder, if the Israelites had been a seafaring nation, whether the rock would have been so decisively an image of protection and safety rather than of peril or menace. For indeed our own habits of usage involve images that associate the rock with danger and trouble. When a ship runs on the rocks it is broken; and we say a man is "on the rocks" when he is financially broken. Contrasting associations of the word *rock* are no more remarkable than are those of *water* and *fire*. One can find places in the Old Testament where the word is given a harsh connotation. "They have made their faces harder than a rock," we read in Jeremiah (5:3) of those who are stubbornly unrepentant. But a prevalent Biblical connotation of the word remains that of firmness and protectiveness. "The Lord is my rock, and my fortress, and my deliverer," says David in his psalm of thanksgiving after battle (2 Sm 22:1). The rock is the refuge of the conies for the psalmist. Our Lord made a distinction between the wise man who built his house upon a rock and the foolish man who built his upon sand (Mt 7:24-27). And of course this was much more than an interesting piece of moral advice about laying proper foundations for whatever you try to build. Christ himself is the rock and his church is built upon it.

Paradox is again evident in the biblical use of the word *stone* (and *stony*). The New Testament image of Christ as the cornerstone or foundation stone is rooted in Old Testament prophecy, such as the psalmist's words, "The stone which the builders refused is become the headstone of the corner" (Ps 118:22) and Isaiah's words, "Therefore thus said the Lord God, 'Behold, I lay in Zion for a foundation a stone, a tried stone, a precious cornerstone, a sure foundation'" (Is 28:16). Yet often enough in the Old Testament a stone is something with which you smite someone, something which hurts you either because it is sharp under your feet or because you accidentally dash your foot against it. So stony places are uncomfortable places, the stony heart is an unfeeling one, and in the parable of the sower the "stony places" on which the seed falls can bring forth no lasting fruit.

In his poem "Sepulchre" George Herbert describes how Christ's own body was thrown into a sepulchre of stone because there had been no open hearts to receive him.

> O blessed body whither art thou thrown?
> No lodging for Thee but cold hard stone!
> So many hearts on earth, and yet not one
>   Receive Thee!

Our hearts give lodging to sins by the score and to trivialities by the thousand, Herbert goes on to say. Yet they leave Christ outside. Indeed our hearts have virtually hit Christ about the head with the stone of sin ("our hearts have took up stones to brain Thee"). Then Herbert draws an illuminating parallel. Just as the old law of the Ten Commandments was written on stone, so Christ, the "letter of the Word," has to be chiseled on to cold hard stone in being imprinted on our hearts.

Christina Rossetti also took up the theme of the heart's

stoniness in a little poem called "Good Friday" in which she compared herself to a stone for being able to contemplate Christ's cross without weeping.

> Am I a stone and not a sheep
> That I can stand, O Christ, beneath Thy Cross
> To number drop by drop Thy Blood's slow loss,
> And yet not weep?

What is especially interesting about this poem is that Christina Rossetti goes on to compare herself to the rock in the wilderness. It had to be smitten before water flowed from it; and she herself is so stonily insensitive that she will have to be smitten before her tears will flow.

> Yet give not o'er,
> But seek Thy Sheep, true Shepherd of the flock;
> Greater than Moses, turn and look once more
> And smite a rock.

There is irony in the fact that Moses was given the miraculous power to strike the rock in answer to a prayer he made out of fear that the Israelites were about to stone him (Ex 17:4). Stoning was an all too familiar form of vengeance and punishment in Old Testament times. "Thou shalt stone him with stones, that he die" (Dt 13:10). Such was the penalty the old law laid down for apostasy, and for adultery too. This law was invoked by the scribes and Pharisees who brought to Jesus a woman who had been taken in adultery; invoked, of course, in the hope of catching him out. He answered them with wisdom and cunning. "He that is without sin among you, let him first cast a stone at her" (Jn 8:7). In this connection we may recall that the first Christian martyr of all, Stephen, was stoned to death. We may also recall the occasion when Jesus himself was all but stoned. The Jews tackled him about his status and authority, and when Jesus was pushed into a corner by some straight questions (Who do you think you are? Are you pretending to be greater than Abraham?) he was ultimately provoked to a straight answer: "Verily, verily I say unto you, before Abraham was, I am" (Jn 8:58). This simple, direct admission of his own authority was what his listeners then, as so often since, could not stomach. "Then took they up stones to cast at him" (Jn 8:59).

A rock is a natural thing, part of the natural environment given to us. Stones, too, are in the first place natural: but a cornerstone, or any other stone with which you build a house or a temple is a human artifact. It has been hewn from the rock of the quarry and cut by human hands—or by the machinery which human hands have made.

I live in an area of "dry-stone walling." The walls around the fields have been built without cement. Moreover they have been built by simply collecting the stones lying about and piling them one on top of another. It is of course a very skilled workman who can do this job properly. He does not cut the stones: he just arranges them so that the finished wall looks as though the stones big and small, round and square, fat and thin, have been haphazardly assembled. In fact the verticality and firmness of the wall prove that the arrangement, stone by stone, has been very carefully thought out. But you could not build a cathedral by the same method. This has to be remembered when reading St. Paul's comparison of Christian men and women to material that must be "builded together for an habitation of God" (Eph 2:22). He sees the whole "household of God" as "built upon the foundation of the apostles and prophets, Jesus Christ himself being the chief corner stone." It is in Christ that "all the building fitly framed together groweth into an holy temple in the Lord" (Eph 2:20-21). Fitly framing involves something more than cunning arrangement: it involves cutting and chiseling and chipping too.

Why do we in this way pursue connections between one use of a word and another? In the first place, to shed light on the power and richness of words themselves—the sheer load of meaning they can carry. In the second place, to shed light on the world around us and how it has been involved, object by object, in the Christian revelation. This tree, that stone, this river, that rock—they or their like have been used by God and used too by his enemies. They carry their message, their history, their load of associations for us. The poet Francis Thompson, something of a mystic, was acutely conscious of the way the unseen world impinges on the seen world, the way signs of the world we cannot fully know here and now can be glimpsed among the things about us. We have no need to search the stars and the vast regions of space in the desire to contact the untouchable world of God's presence. The evidence is all about us. We shall not make contact with God's angels by mentally (or physically) exploring the outer universe. The sweep of angelic wings, Thompson says, is all about us, were we not too clogged by earthiness to hear them. And he adds this remarkable line: "Turn but a stone and start a wing."

That is what this study is all about. Turn a stone over and you may disturb an angel. Or look at a fire. Or stare at a river. Or let the tap water trickle through your fingers. Do these things meditatively. And next time you climb a rock, think of all that the rock stands for. Next time you see a building being built, think of how we Christians are all being built, brick by brick, into the fabric of God's temple, a habitation for himself.

For it is only a literary device that this book appears to be about words. It is really about life. And not just life in the past, but life in the present too. For words enable us to bring the experiences of past and present together. We are not concerned only with the stones that prevented the sower's seeds from being fruitful or the stones thrown at St. Stephen. We are concerned with the stones at your feet in your garden. You can pick one of them up tomorrow and hurl it at our Lord for making the absurd claim to be divine. There is one thing, however, that you will surely not do. When dinner time comes round and your children are seated expectantly at the table, you will not pick that stone up, carry it inside, deposit it on the table before your children's eyes and say, "Eat that. It's all you're going to get." You won't do that. You might throw a stone at our Lord in the form of a sin (as George Herbert put it). But you won't give a stone to your own children for food. Jesus himself knew in advance that you wouldn't. "Or what man is there of you, whom if his son ask bread, will he give him a stone?" (Mt 7:9). And he went on to add: If you, however evil you are, stop short of denying good things to your children, how much more surely will God your Father in heaven give good things to you if you ask for them.

Some stones are themselves precious. The priestly breastplate described in Exodus (28:17-20) is to have four rows of precious stones, three in each row, to represent the twelve tribes of Israel. And the foundations of the wall of the heavenly New Jerusalem described in the book of Revelation are also garnished with precious stones. If the children of Israel under the old dispensation could be accounted so many precious stones, then we Christians, by virtue of the calling that we should be built together into the habitation of God, have the right to hope that, stone by stone, we shall be precious in his sight. Indeed we know that we are precious. Two sparrows are sold for a farthing, Christ said, and yet neither of them could fall to the ground without the Father's knowledge. "Fear ye not therefore, ye are of more value than many sparrows" (Mt 10:31). We are stones. And we are precious.

EIGHT

Blood

W HEN WE ARE DRIVING merrily along the highway and are suddenly pulled up by the police and catch sight of a battered car at the roadside or lying on its side in a field nearby, our mood is transformed. We see the flickering lights of the ambulances, we see people bending over a human body lying on the grass or perhaps even in the road. It is all very upsetting. It fills us with apprehension. But the terror and the shrinking are always intensified if we catch sight of a scarlet stain—a pool of blood in the road or a reddened shirt. When I was a young child, in much earlier motoring days in the interwar years, I remember how we once set out on a beautiful bank holiday for a picnic on the moors. My father and mother sat in the front of the car. We children sat in the back. Driving up a long hill we suddenly came across one of the saddest sights I have ever seen. A man had been leading his horse and cart from a side road into the main road. A vehicle coming racing down the hill had just collided with him and his horse. It must have happened but a moment or two before we drove up. The horse lay in the road. The man who had been leading it, who (as we read in the local newspaper that same evening) died very soon afterwards, was as yet not dead. Worse still, as it seemed to me as a child, he was not yet even stretched on the ground, but with a mass of blood for a face he was *sitting*. My father drove past out of concern for us children, then parked the car and went back to see what could be done. The holiday outing was ruined, of course. It was possible to forget the incident fitfully, but it kept recurring to the mind. And since I am now writing about what happened over fifty years later, I do not need to explain that the picture of that man with the smashed and bloodied face has stayed with me ever since—though I could not say another word about anything else that happened that day. I cannot even remember where we went, what we did, or even whether all the family were with us. Only one thing has survived in the mind through the years since—the image of a man sitting in the middle of the road with a mass of blood for a face and a horse lying behind him.

So powerful is the image of blood. Yet one cannot write or speak about Christ's death on the cross and what it meant for the human race without using the word *blood*. The phrase "the blood of Christ" occurs more often in the New Testament than the phrase "the death of Christ." Violent death so often involves bloodletting that we use the word *bloodshed* when speaking of slaughter in war even though—as, I suppose, for the victims of Hiroshima or the Nazi gas ovens—some of the worst horrors may be comparatively bloodless. Murder has always been regarded by our legal systems as the greatest crime. The taking of life has always been regarded as the ultimate punishment. The flow of blood is such a sure indication of the ebbing away of life that we naturally speak of people who die in defense of their country or some other cause as shedding their blood for others. The treatment of Christ being what it was, he bled inevitably—from the scourged back, the crowned head, the pierced side, and the nailed hands and feet. Metaphorically and literally too this was a great shedding of blood for others.

In the twentieth century, for the first time in history, it is possible to give your blood for others without dying. Blood donors generously allow themselves to be tapped so that others who might otherwise die from loss or infection of their own blood can be restored to health. This practice sheds a new light on Christ's act of self-sacrifice and on the concept of blood freely given for others. Christ gave so much blood that he died. But the unfailing blood bank he thereby endowed and stocked became a source of healing for the human race forever afterward. We know that for the Jews of Old Testament days a solemn covenant was sealed by animal sacrifice and by the sprinkling of blood. When God gave the Hebrews the law by which they were to live and the people gave their pledge of acceptance, Moses sacrificed oxen to God and sprinkled the blood, half on the altar and half on the people themselves, saying, "Behold the blood of the covenant, which the Lord hath made with you concerning all these words" (Ex 24:8). It was in keeping therefore with the most solemn Hebrew tradition that a new covenant between God and his people should be sealed by the sacrifice of a victim and the sprinkling of the victim's blood on the people. It is interesting that in the traditional Christian imagery of Christ's blood being thereafter available to all men and women for their healing and their regeneration we find an anticipation of the notion of a blood bank upon which all stricken people can call for a life-saving injection. The notion is of a human blood stream infected by the stain of Adam's sin and by all subsequent sinfulness; and the infection is one which only the blood of a man of unsullied humanity can counter and cleanse. Mercifully, the divine blood bank stocked by Christ is itself uninfectable. Human blood banks, alas, are not so. We know that from the way AIDS sufferers can convey their fatal disease to others by donating their blood. It might be difficult to find an apter illustration of the way the infection of evil can poison the human bloodstream than the transmission of AIDS. Indeed original sin is a kind of inescapable spiritual AIDS—Adam's Immunity-Destruction Sin—by inheritance exposing us, without adequate defenses, to the ubiquitous infections of evil. There is only one known antidote.

That Christ himself meant us to think of his blood as shed for the healing of us all is evident from what he did at the Last

Supper. Having given the disciples the bread to eat and declaring it his own body, broken for them, he then gave them wine to drink saying, "This cup is the new testament (covenant) in my blood; this do ye, as oft as ye drink it, in remembrance of me" (1 Cor 11:25).

The pervasiveness of blood is what makes it such an apt symbol. Blood circulates through the entire body, dancing through every artery and vein. This movement of blood is the very basis of continuing human life. Blood is pervasive in another way too. "There is blood on his hands," we say of a murderer, implying that the stain is one which cannot be removed. After Lady Macbeth has played her part in the murder of King Duncan in her home, she can never again feel that her hands are clean. This is what haunts her in nightmares so that she roams the castle in her sleep in the middle of the night, desperately trying to wash her hands. Hers is a delirium of permanently bloodied fingers and palms. The all-pervasiveness of the murdered victim's blood is torment to those who have wilfully acquiesced in his murder, whether the victim be Shakespeare's King Duncan or Jesus Christ. But the great paradox of Christ's self-sacrifice is that to those who partake of it in fellowship with him, his blood is blood that cleanses, not stains: it is health and salvation instead of torment and guilt.

In his *Four Quartets* T.S. Eliot has a number of verses which picture the human race as patients in a hospital.

The whole earth is our hospital . . .

Here we are, lying on sickbeds, diseased, indeed sick unto death. Eliot pictures Christ as our surgeon, but he is himself a "wounded surgeon" and he bends over us with "bleeding hands" to give us the painful treatment our condition requires. He "plies the steel" which probes our own wounds. Meanwhile our nurse, the church, takes care of us, not trying to "please" us with false consolations, but reminding us of our desperate condition. We need to accept that condition. For the paradox is that this is a hospital in which we must "die" in order to "do well." So we shiver and burn in the extremes of feverishness:

The dripping blood our only drink,
The bloody flesh our only food.

Here is an image of humanity as a suffering body which expresses the truths of our fallen condition and of Christ's sacrifice and atonement in terms of a modern hospital ward and an operating theater. The word "dripping" might suggest that the patient is on an intravenous drip. Indeed, that is exactly the situation of Christians. All Christians are on a drip. We have all been connected up to the life-support system which Christ's sacrifice set up. His church is a massive intensive-care unit. Thus Christian doctrine, like all truth, becomes clearer and more meaningful, not by removing metaphor, but by strengthening and, where necessary, updating it.

It is perhaps not surprising that blood-red sunsets have sometimes called to people's minds the suffering of Christ. To see, right across the heaven above us, the sweep of scarlet overspreading our world, is to recall how the whole world lies under the protection of Christ's sacrifice. In Marlowe's play *Dr. Faustus* the hero sells his soul to the Devil in order to win back years of youth and pleasure. At the end, when his time is up, and the Devil arrives to claim his share of the bargain and drag his victim off to Hell, Faustus cries out in desperation:

See, see where Christ's blood streams in the firmament!
One drop would save my soul, half a drop; ah, my Christ!

Another poet, F.T. Prince, a young English officer in the Second World War, watched his men bathing one day and pondered war's burden of horror and bloodshed:

> while in the west
> I watch a streak of red that might have issued from Christ's
> breast.

In more senses than one blood is what binds people together. "They are of our own blood," we say of our kith and kin. Blood-relationships are the closest and most we have. And we are all blood-relations of Christ. Moreover blood carries overtones of quality. There's nothing like "blood" to give the stamp of quality to any living species, human or animal. Certainly nothing like the blood of Christ, the supreme blood royal. St. John's great vision of heaven pictures the saved arrayed in white robes, and the elder says of them, "These are they which came out of great tribulation, and have washed their robes, and made them white in the blood of the Lamb" (Rv 7:14).

NINE

Wine

The King sits in Dunfermline town
Drinking the blood-red wine.

THAT IS HOW THE OLD BALLAD of Sir Patrick Spens begins. The imaginative connection between blood and wine is a settled one in literature. When Macbeth tells the two sons of King Duncan that their father is dead, he declares that the "source" and "fountain" of their blood has been dammed up. But shortly afterwards he adopts a different image for the drying up of Duncan's stream of life.

The wine of life is drawn, and the mere lees
Is left . . .

Duncan's blood having been shed, the cask of wine is empty; only the undrinkable lees remain.

Now it so happens that such talk in *Macbeth* has its highly ironic side. Macbeth may like to think that a fountain of blood has been securely plugged. And he may like to picture to himself a cask of rich red wine which has finally run dry. But Lady Macbeth sees things differently. "Here's the smell of blood still," she moans, wringing her hands as she walks in her sleep. "All the perfumes of Arabia will not sweeten this little hand." And she cries a cry of tragic despair. "Who would have thought the old man to have had so much blood in him!"

For the Christian this imagery of blood and wine is among the most moving things in Shakespeare. Especially so because Duncan himself is pictured as a saintly person of great virtue and piety, truly representing in his kingship the divine authority on earth. Macbeth, on the other hand, gripped by the devilry of the weird sisters and urged on by his wife, murders his king when the king comes to visit him, as mankind murdered Christ.

There was no plugging the fountain of blood which Christ's crucifixion released. A thousand hymns and prayers remind us of how it has continued to flow. The great cask of wine was not emptiable. It is there to be drawn upon still.

Christ did not in this connection compare himself to anything so lifeless as a wine barrel. He compared himself to a living vine. "I am the true vine, and my Father is the husbandman," he said (Jn 15:1), and later, "I am the vine, ye are the branches" (Jn 15:5). The branches of the vine can bear fruit only if the sap of the vine flows through them. If this flow ceases, the branch withers and is good for nothing but to be burned. If the flow is maintained the branch will be fruitful. The images of the vine and the vineyard were traditionally used to represent the Israelites as a whole. The psalmist declares, "Thou hast brought a vine out of Egypt; thou hast cast out the heathen, and planted it" (Ps 80:8). The first remarkable thing about Christ's use of the image is that he declares himself alone the "true vine" of which his disciples are branches. And the second remarkable thing about it is that Christ thus anticipates the use of the fruit of the vine as the symbol of his blood. The offering of the cup at the Last Supper extends the range of the vine imagery. As the life-giving sap flows through the branches, so the wine which is Christ's blood is forever an offer to be partaken of in recollection of his death.

The sheer "naturalness" of Christian imagery is inescapable. Imagery can be illuminating without being "natural." When John Donne took leave of his wife on one occasion, he wrote a poem comparing their relationship in love to a pair of compasses. I have to go away, he said. You stay at home, like the fixed arm of the compass. I roam away from you like the arm which draws the circle. But the circle will be a true one only in so far as you lean out towards me and follow my every movement. And we shall be securely united again when my task is done only if you stick your ground firmly at the center to which I must return. This is certainly an illuminating image as well as an ingenious one. It provokes thought. It arouses admiration for its cleverness. But it is not "natural" in the sense that it can take its place among a series of connections that together shed increasing light on aspects of our life. You cannot move forward from the image of the compasses to comparable connecting images involving pencils and T-squares, erasers and drawing boards. At least you cannot move "naturally" through such a series of connections. A mind like Donne's might fabricate related images by the exercise of determined ingenuity, but they would not link together as the Christian imagery of blood and wine, vine and branch link together. Artifically contrived imagery is never "inevitable." It does not make you say, "Why, of course!" Instead it makes you say, "How clever! I should never have thought of that." It is not imagery which is so infectious that forever afterwards you find people comparing parted lovers to the extended arms of compasses. But once the imagery of blood and wine, vine and branch has taken root in the mind of the Christian, it grows and itself bears fruit.

The English novelist T.F. Powys lived in a small village in Dorset, secluded from the busy world, and contemplated the lives of the people in the rural community, noting with equal precision the virtues of the good and the savageries and lusts of the bad. In his finest novel, *Mr. Weston's Good Wine*, he pictured a divine visitation to a village one winter evening. Time stands still and the villagers come under judgment. But God does not come to the village in glory or even in the guise of a saintly prophet. He comes in a Ford delivery van as a traveling wine merchant, Mr. Weston, and his assistant is appropriately given the angelic name "Michael." Mr. Weston has two brands of wine to offer, the Light Wine which is Love and whose price is the return of Love, and the Dark Wine which is Death and whose price is life itself. The two wines are one. And there is no human trouble that it cannot cure.

In blessing the cup and giving it to his disciples at the Last Supper our Lord conferred a special mystique on the cup which held the wine. We have mentioned already the connection which was to be made later between the cup in which Christ's blood was made available and the womb in which he was carried before birth. In the Middle Ages legends grew around the "Holy Grail." This was supposed to be the cup used by Christ at the Last Supper. Legend had it that Joseph of Arimathea took possession of the cup and that later he came to England with it and built a church at Glastonbury. Glastonbury Abbey was certainly one of the oldest monasteries in England and various legends associated Joseph of Arimathea, King Arthur, and St. Patrick with it. The Holy Grail became a powerful symbol, not only because it was the cup used at the Last Supper, but also because it was said to have been used to receive Christ's blood when he was put on the cross. It was consequently assumed to have mystic properties. Miracles were performed in its presence, but since its whereabouts were wrapped in mystery the quest to find it became a key theme of medieval romance, a theme taken up in the stories that gathered around King Arthur and his Round Table.

This might seem to be a topic too fanciful and too wrapped about with superstition to be dwelled upon here, were it not that the Holy Grail quest as represented in our literature called out great achievements of heroic sanctity and self-discipline and kept its power to inspire poets and writers up to our own age. Wagner used the topic in his last opera, *Parsifal*. The Christian poet Charles Williams returned to it in his two sequences of Arthurian poems, *Taliessin through Logres* and *The Region of the Summer Stars*. The Grail is the symbol on which expectations of the return of our Lord are focused. Moreover, the cup as a prize at the end of a testing quest remains a feature of our lives today. We still award silver cups as trophies to mark fine achievements. A "cup holder" or "cup winner" is someone who has distinguished himself or herself, generally by the strenuous attainment of excellence. Perhaps we ought not to be able to hear of cups awarded for this or that without turning our thoughts to *the* Cup of which all other such trophies are copies.

We eat and drink daily, and it is significant that so much Christian symbolism has gathered around the simplest acts of daily living and some of the simplest objects of daily use. In a sense it is a guarantee of Christian truth that wherever you turn you find Christian teachings and images relevant and illuminating. As wine, like corn and oil and honey, is an Old Testament symbol of the abundance and richness of God's earthly provisions for his people, so the cup is the vessel in which God's bounty is contained. "My cup runneth over" (Ps 23:5), we sing in the best known of all psalms in praise of God's bounty and mercy. "I will take the cup of salvation, and call upon the name of the Lord" (Ps 116:13) and "The Lord is the portion of mine inheritance and of my cup" (Ps 16:5), the psalmist declares. But the cup which God offers for our eating and drinking is not always a cup of obvious blessings. When our Lord in his agony prayed to God in the Garden of Gethsemane, he cried, "Father, if thou be willing remove this cup from me: nevertheless not my will, but thine, be done" (Lk 22:42).

TEN

Body

THE IMAGE OF THE CHURCH as the body of Christ is linked naturally to the image of Christ as the Vine of which his disciples are branches. St. Paul speaks of Christ as "the head of the body, the church" (Col 1:18), and elsewhere expands this image, declaring that we are "all members of one body in Christ" (Rom 12:4) and that we differ in our gifts and functions as arms, legs, eyes, and ears differ. Yet all are essential to the healthy functioning of the whole.

There is an episode at the beginning of Shakespeare's Roman play, *Coriolanus*, where Menenius Agrippa addresses an angry crowd of mutinous citizens. There is a shortage of food, the price of grain has risen, and the contrast between the well-to-do and well-fed patricians and the famished plebeians has become intolerable. In trying to appease the mob, Menenius narrates a fable. He tells how the rest of the body's members once rebelled against the belly for sticking there inactive in the middle of them all and just receiving food while the rest of them got on with their jobs. The belly defended itself on the grounds that it was the storehouse from which they all drew nourishment, nourishment sent through rivers of blood to heart and brain, nerves and veins. No individual member can see how every other member is benefiting from the belly's deliveries, but in fact it distributes what is necessary to them all. Menenius thus tries to persuade the angry citizens that the senate is like the belly, and they cannot individually appreciate how its services sustain them all.

The image of the body as a collection of human beings has often appealed to thinkers and poets. There is a fine instance of this in Spenser's long poem, *The Faerie Queene*. The second book of the poem concerns the quest of Sir Guyon, the knight of Temperance, whose purpose is to destroy those who corrupt mankind by temptations to intemperance. One of his exploits involves clearing away the evil appetites and vicious desires that beseige the house in which the Virgin Soul dwells. The Virgin Soul is called Alma. Her house, or castle, is the human body in which she lives. Guyon pays her a visit. The castle he enters is pictured in detail as a human body. The gates at the front entry are the mouth, and there is a vine (mustache) trailing over one of them. The portcullis is like a nose. A porter (the tongue) keeps guard within the gates day and night. (His alarm bell can be heard far and wide.) There are two rows of brightly armed warders (the teeth). Guyon goes downwards first into the vault of the stomach with its furnace and its one great chimney carrying hot air upwards. This kitchen is staffed by a cook and his servants. Guyon notes the ventilation system, a huge pair of bellows (the lungs). He also notes (for the Elizabethans were not over-delicate) the efficient system of conduit pipes that get rid of waste at the back door. But what is more subtle is that the heart is a richly decorated parlor in which a bevy of beautiful ladies sit on the floor. They are the feelings. Some laugh, some sing, some trifle, some frown, some fawn, some blush for shame, some are coy, some seem envious. But (for this is a well-regulated household) when Alma, the resident soul, comes in with Guyon, they all stand up together and do homage. They are kept under firm but kind discipline. Guyon is especially interested in a rather sober young lady who represents Desire for Fame and Honor, and another blushful young lady with downcast eyes who is chaste in her dress and bashful in her bearing and who of course represents Modesty. That is the taste you would expect of the knight of Temperance.

Guyon's tour of this dwelling of the Virgin Soul then takes him up a stately turret (the neck). The arched roof of the tower is decked with flowers (hair) and there are two beacons so cunningly made that they swivel in silver sockets: these are the eyes. At the top of the tower are three chambers. In the first (front) one lives Imagination, in the middle one, Reason, and in the rear one, Memory. Each, of course, is appropriately equipped and housed.

The point of this extensive illustration is to show how far-reaching is the image of the body as a symbol of a working community. We still use the word *body* freely, describing a society or a collection of men and women as "a body of people." But in so using the word *body* its strict connotation is all but lost. The word has become an empty label for a collective, and the image of the human body no longer rises to the mind as we use it. This is what linguistic experts call a "dead metaphor." Our daily conversation is packed with "dead metaphors," even our most casual colloquialisms. "He's barking up the wrong tree," we say without mentally picturing him as a yelping dog or even conceptualizing a tree. "She laughed her head off," we say, but no horrific picture of self-inflicted decapitation impinges on the mind. Or quite apart from such highly colored traditional sayings, we remark that it was an "arid discussion" without registering the true physical quality of aridity, or that it was a "heated discussion" without registering physical warmth. And I may speak of "freezing a project" without the merest hint of a shiver in the mind.

It is the business of poets to give us new metaphors. It is also the business of poets to revitalize old metaphors. Quotations from the poets in this book are intended to show these processes at work.

One of the saddest things about theological writing in the past twenty-five years has been the loss of imaginative sensitivity to words. I do not know of a single liberal theologian who has shown the kind of sensitivity to words which is natural to men and women of a literary turn of mind. When Christian teachers tell us that the church "is the Body of Christ," we must not allow the metaphor to be drained of meaning. The preservation of the Christian faith in all its fullness and richness depends upon resisting the draining off of meaning. Liberal theologians, if you let them, will go through a lush verbal and conceptual countryside and leave it looking like a dustbowl. Common carelessness in the use of words enables them to do this and to get away with it. To a certain extent this carelessness is inevitable. We say, "The United Nations is a body set up to do this or that," or "The British Medical Association is a body set up to do this or that" and "body" is a drained, anemic label. In the sphere of theology we Christians have to resist the decay that leaves words as empty shells. The church is the body of Christ—and a thousand enlightenments depend upon our sensitivity to what a body is, to what Christ's body in particular was subjected to, and to what he himself said of it in handing bread to his disciples.

Spenser's elaborate picture of the House of Temperance in which the Virgin Soul dwells is obviously in tune with St. Paul's declaration, "Your body is the temple of the Holy Ghost" (1 Cor 6:19). In Spenser's poem, when Guyon has departed from the House of Temperance it is finally assaulted by all the deadly sins and vices. The strategy is carefully planned, and the five great bulwarks of the castle—the senses of sight, hearing, smell, taste, and touch—are assailed by specialized troops. Above all, a bestial being of satanic evil and horror, the incarnation of all vicious passions, makes his appearance. Alma's house is in dire danger. Only one person is capable of dealing with the monster and that is Prince Arthur, who represents Christ. Even he is all but broken by the ferocity of the conflict. In defeating the monster he is gravely wounded, loses a lot of blood, but is carried to where he can be treated "with balm and wine, and costly spicery," laid in a bed, and his wound dressed by Alma.

In the same way the wounded Christ takes over the assaulted human body and makes it his dwelling, his temple. He himself described his own human body as a temple. "Destroy this temple, and in three days I will raise it up," he said, and John explains, "But he spake of the temple of his body" (Jn 2:19, 21).

ELEVEN

Bread

"I AM THE LIVING BREAD which came down from heaven,"
Jesus said. "If any man eat of this bread, he shall live for
ever: and the bread that I will give is my flesh, which I will give
for the life of the world." The Jews quite naturally argued
among themselves about this extraordinary statement. How
on earth can this fellow give up his flesh to eat? And Jesus
reiterated the point. "Whoso eateth my flesh, and drinketh my
blood, hath eternal life." Indeed, he repeated it a third time.
"He that eateth my flesh, and drinketh my blood, dwelleth in
me, and I in him" (Jn 6:51-56).

This was one of those instances where Jesus didn't really
leave us in much doubt. You're not grappling with something
rather abstract or abstruse—like, say, the doctrine of the
Trinity—when you turn to the subject of Jesus as the bread of
life. It may be a mystifying matter in some ways. But it doesn't
tax the imagination like trying to picture the Holy Spirit or
wondering how angels fill their time (or their eternity). We all
know what bread is. Bread is the staff of life. Everyone we
know eats it. But they don't ostensibly eat anyone's flesh or
drink his blood. Such a practice would turn them into
something more than bewildering eccentrics in the eyes of
others.

R.S. Thomas, perhaps the greatest living English poet, has
spent his life as a parish priest ministering to the villagers and

hill-farmers of rural Wales. His devotion to this work and his refusal to be lionized as a literary figure have made him one of the most respected literary people of our age. In one poem, "The Priest," he pictures the parson picking his way through his parish. People's eyes are on him from the windows of the farms. He wonders what others might make of him as he goes—

> limping through life
> On his prayers. There are other people
> In the world, sitting at table
> Contented, though the broken body
> And the shed blood are not on the menu.

This is one of the distinguishing marks of Christians then. The broken body and the shed blood are on their menu.

There is something presumptuous in having the divine body and blood on one's menu. The more vividly you try to realize what it means, to eat your Lord's flesh and drink his blood, the more outrageous it seems. But an order is an order; and Christ made this particular order very clear indeed. Have we the right to turn aside—even on the very sure ground of our unworthiness? This issue was tackled in verse long ago by an earlier priest-poet than R.S. Thomas, by George Herbert who ministered in a little parish near Salisbury. He compressed into a few lines a dialogue between himself and Christ that is packed with meaning. Christ is welcoming him, as it were, at the door of his own house; and naturally he hangs back, aware of how sinful he is. Christ is quick to notice his reluctance and gently asks him if there is something he wants. He replies that only one thing is lacking and that is a guest who is worthy to be welcomed here. "But you shall be the guest," Christ says. "Me, with all my sins of unkindness and ingratitude? I can't even look you in the face." At this Christ takes his hand with a smile and asks, "And was it not I who made those eyes and gave you them?" "Of course, Lord, but I have misused them. I'm ashamed to be here. Let me go elsewhere." "But don't you know," Christ says, "who it is who bore the guilt?" This so convinces the guest that he yields. "I will come in then, but I insist on serving at table." Even that is not permitted. This is how the argument ends:

> "You must sit down," says Love, "and taste My meat."
> So I did sit and eat.

Remember how Christ introduced the parable he told about the man who prepared a festive supper and, when the day came, the guests all began to excuse themselves, apologizing for not being able to come. So the host sent his servants out into the streets and roads to fill up the tables with any beggars or riffraff they could find. Christ introduced this parable by saying, "Blessed is he that shall eat bread in the kingdom of God" (Lk 14:15). There is a compulsive hospitality here as there was in George Herbert's fable. Of course the invited guests in the parable are very different from the guest in Herbert's poem. In the parable the guests' reluctance to go to the feast is due to the fact that they have other things to do. Their other concerns preoccupy them: they're just not interested in the proffered feast. But in Herbert's poem the guest's reluctance is due simply to his knowledge of his own unworthiness of so great an honor. The one kind of reluctance angers the host so that he vows that the guests who have rejected his invitation shall never taste a meal of his. The other kind of reluctance provokes the gentle pressure of reassurance from the host and the friendly but firm instruction to sit and eat. In St. John's vision in the book of Revelation the supper is given a mystical status. It has become the marriage feast of the Lamb. "Blessed are they which are called unto the marriage supper of the Lamb" (Rev 19:9).

Jesus described the kingdom of heaven as being "like unto leaven which a woman took and hid in three measures of meal, till the whole was leavened" (Mt 13:33). The image of leavening is an expressive one. In Shakespeare's *Measure for Measure* the Duke tells Angelo that he is putting him in charge of Vienna during his absence. When Angelo protests that he may not be equal to the task, the Duke says:

> No more evasion:
> We have with a leavened and prepared choice
> Proceeded to you.

In other words, "We have chosen you after a very carefully pondered selection process." *Leavened* here means "thoroughly thought out." The leaven is the core of weighty reasoning behind the decision. This use of the word *leaven* for the central animating element in a matter is like our Lord's usage. There is a moving poem, "Hospital for Defectives," by the English poet Thomas Blackburn that extends this usage. Blackburn has told how he came to write the poem. One day he saw some mental defectives from a hospital working in a turnip field. "Some of them pulled and pushed a cart and one had the job of catching turnips and placing them in the cart after the warder had slashed off the top leaves with a large knife. Something was tickling his nose and he kept muffing his catches. After a while the officer lost his patience and slapped the man three times across the mouth." What impressed Blackburn especially was the response—or lack of response— of the defective, who neither winced nor cried out. He "just stood still in the pouring rain, his white face lifted upward." This distressing spectacle left Blackburn bewildered. "What is it that can make something as beautiful as an eyelid and as terrible as a hydrocephalic idiot?" He asks the question—not in order to discredit God or to challenge God, but with that agony of bafflement which the spectacle of suffering and the conviction of God's love together inevitably prompt. After all, Blackburn seems to say, God's love is made evident in the beauty of a face or a flower, and many things around us seem to reflect the "stirrings" of the divine heart; then in what way do these men in the turnip field speak of God's love? Two men pick up turnips, two men pull the cart,

> And yet between the four of them
> No word is ever said
> Because the yeast was not put in
> Which makes the human bread.

It is their wordlessness that seems to signify their condition as yeastless, defective human bread (and we must remember that there is "wordlessness" and "Word-less-ness" too).

> Beneath the warder's blows
> The unleavened man did not cry out
> Or turn his face away . . .

Blackburn addresses God directly:

> Through such men in a turnip field
> What is it that you say?

The question is one which Christians ask of God in all ages. If they do not ask it, they must be unfeeling creatures indeed, for there is human suffering all around us. But what more directly concerns us here is that Blackburn sees the created world in terms of the utterance of God. What is God saying in this or that revelation? God in his loves makes a language which men can read in the beauty of a face or a rose. God speaks to us in these revelations. And it is the speechlessness of the defectives which shows that they lack the leaven to make them healthy human bread. What is memorable here is that the leavening of the otherwise mindless lump of human dough is seen as needful for the utterance of the word—the power to receive and voice the word. The word, of course, is perhaps the richest of all Christian symbols.

TWELVE

Door and Key

W HEN CHRIST DECLARED he was the vine, he was comparing himself to a growing, living thing. When he called
the bread and wine his body and his blood, he was identifying
himself with products of the living world which nourish and
refresh human beings. But surprisingly perhaps, he also
compared himself to inanimate objects. "I am the way," he
said. Now in English the word *way* is used in a variety of ways
(*sic*). We say, "I do not like her ways" or "The ways of God are
strange" and the word means something rather abstract like
"habits" or "practices." But when Christ said, "I am the way,
the truth, and the life," he went on to add "No man cometh to
the Father but by me" (Jn 14:6). Plainly he had in mind a road
or a path that leads one to a destination.

We are more likely to compare people to inanimate objects
unflatteringly than in compliment. "He's a clod," we say, or
"He's as deaf as a post." But not content with comparing
himself to a road, Christ also compared himself to a door or
gate. He reminded his disciples that a thief would climb a fence
to get into a sheepfold, but a shepherd would go in by the
door. Then, before going on to compare himself with the good
shepherd, he compared himself to the door of the fold
through which the sheep go safely in and out to seek shelter or
pasture. "I am the door: by me if any man enter in, he shall be
saved, and shall go in and out, to find pasture" (Jn 10:9).

I once knew a young schoolteacher who was quite keen on getting the children he taught to perform little playlets in the classroom. One of his devices was to get children to represent the scenery as well as the characters. "You stand here, Ann, and be a tree. That means stretching your arms out like this." "You stand here, Susan, and be a lamppost. That means being absolutely still" (one way of keeping someone immobile). "And you stand here, Jimmy: you're a mailbox. That means keeping your mouth wide open" (a good way of keeping someone quiet). The other children could be amused by such living furniture. The temptation to post a letter in Jimmy's mouth was not always resistible.

I recall these memories because I feel a certain curiosity about how Jesus' audience responded when they heard him temporarily assume the role of a door. Did he add any histrionic touches when he made such comparisons? When he said, "I am the Vine and ye are the branches" did he stretch his arms up in the air and outwards? When he said "I am the door" did he swivel his body as though on a huge hinge? Or did he just stand with arms out to left and right, imitating a barrier that no one was going to pass without his permission? Whatever he did, it is interesting that, according to the gospel, he was soon describing himself as the good shepherd. In the text that has reached us the transition is swift. I suppose, translated into modern terms, it was rather like saying, "I am the security check: no one can take a flight to the Father without going through me," and the next moment adding, "I am the Good Pilot: the Good Pilot cares for his passengers and will fly them safely to their destination." The latter comparison seems fitter than the former. It is more natural to picture Christ as the pilot who controls the vessel that carries you than to picture him as a rectangular frame which will give off a bleep if you go through it with a revolver in your pocket. But it might be salutary for us to remember that Christ's image of himself as the door allowing only selective ingress is not unlike a security check. It would be easier for a camel to go through the needle's eye than for a rich man to enter the kingdom of God (Lk 18:25). We all know these days that the "needle's eye" was the name of a very narrow gateway and that makes our comparison apt. It might be easier for a passenger to get through the security check with his pockets stuffed with krugerrands than for a rich man to enter into the kingdom of God.

There is a great deal of flexibility in the use of imagery in the Bible. In the book of Revelation, God is the one who knocks on the door of the human heart, seeking admission. "Behold, I stand at the door and knock: if any man hear my voice, and open the door, I will come in to him and will sup with him, and he with me" (Rv 3:20). This usage of the image complements the other one. In this case the door is the barrier that keeps God from man or the means of entry that brings God to man. In the other case the door is the barrier that keeps man from God or the means of approach that brings man to God. The one door gives entry into God's keeping as a member of his flock: the other door is a house door and brings God into the center of daily life at the dinner table.

Imagery of gates had a richer public significance in the days when cities were walled and gated. Nevertheless the image of the wide gate and the broad road leading to destruction and of the narrow gate and way leading to eternal life is still full of relevance. We may think of the wide gates opened to let a great crowd out of a football field and the narrow turnstiles before which people must line up and through which they must pass in single file, one by one, when going in. No doubt when journeys involved going in and out of city gates, and later still when roads were cut into sections by turnpikes and tollgates, the imagery of a gate as an obstacle or an aid to progress was more constantly in mind. Not that open gates are always generally welcome. Prison gates keep dangerous men where they can do no damage to others. And when Christ called Peter the rock on which he would build his church, he added, "The gates of hell shall not prevail against it" (Mt 16:18). The word *hell* is used in the King James Bible to translate two quite different words, one of which means the abode of the dead generally rather than of the wicked, and that is the usage here. However, gates are barriers whether they are keeping out enemies or friends, whether they are keeping in criminals or innocent people. And the message that death is an ineffective barrier against the church is simple and straightforward enough. But the mention of the rock on one side and the gates of death on the other side conjures up the picture of two rival fortresses. That is the image that tends to present itself when one hears the passage read aloud in church. The gates of hell are gates through which the forces of death and destruction can scarcely break out to ravage the country around. And if they do break out and swarm over the surrounding terrain, they are powerless against the church, towering impregnably above them. I suspect that this somewhat fanciful picture owes something to the modern practice of using the word *gate* in the sense of a large concourse of people attending a ball-game. ("There was a record gate at last Saturday's match.")

After our Lord told St. Peter that the gates of hell should not prevail against the church, he went on to say, "And I will give unto thee the keys of the kingdom of heaven" (Mt 16:19). It is interesting that the image of the gates of hell is so quickly replaced by the image of the gates of heaven—though the word *gates* is not in fact used in reference to heaven, only the word *keys*. The statement is one of the most remarkable that Christ made. A mortal man is being told that he shall hold the keys of the eternal kingdom and that whatever he forbids or allows on earth, those decisions will hold good in heaven too. Keys empower one to open a gate or a door and go inside. In the case of the kingdom of heaven getting inside or not getting inside is the difference between salvation and damnation, between everlasting life and death. Control of the keys is a matter of almost unthinkable power and authority.

In our own day we tend to think of a modestly placed person—perhaps a janitor or a caretaker—as the one who looks after the keys of a building. But of course such a key-holder acts only in obedience to someone in authority in whom the real power of the keys resides. The bank manager is responsible for the keys to the bank's strongrooms and safes. Perhaps the aptest contemporary parallel to the power of the keys given into the care of St. Peter might be the nuclear key entrusted into the care of the president of the United States. There indeed is power over life and death for millions of the world's inhabitants. Yet this power over life and death of human beings is but power to delay or hasten a death which must come to all human beings sooner or later anyway. When one tries to imagine, by comparison, how mighty is the holder of the key which gives power over the granting or the denying of eternal life to mortal men and women, the mind boggles.

In connection with the image of the key it should be remembered that what the psalmist called a "headstone" we call a "keystone"—the stone inserted at the top of an arch which keeps the rest in place. When Jesus quoted the psalmist, "The stone which the builders rejected, the same is become the head of the corner" (Mt 21:42), he gave us the image of himself as the keystone of the arch. This bringing together of the images of the key and the stone reminds us how Christ brought together the images of the rock and the keys in his words to St. Peter.

We use the word *key* very freely today for levers and buttons that enable the fingers to manipulate machinery—a typewriter for instance. We also use the word for the keys of a piano or an organ. Such usages tend to weaken the word, in that we picture rows of keys all alike on the keyboard or almost all alike on the typewriter. But nevertheless we use the word too in a sense which restores great significance to it. "The key to last week's puzzle will be found on page 17," we read in a magazine. "I'm searching for the key to a most difficult problem," we say when we have an issue to be sorted out whose complexities tax and baffle us. "This is the key to the project," we say in triumph when we have an inspired idea for some new scheme or proposal that will solve a lot of practical difficulties and surmount numerous obstacles. St. Peter's keys are thus potent symbols for what answers the gravest problems as well as for what opens the gates of everlasting life.

THIRTEEN

The Way

CHRIST IS THE WAY, and it is natural for us to think of the Christian life as a journey. There are difficulties to be encountered, obstacles to be surmounted en route, but there is a destination, heaven, at the end. John Bunyan's *Pilgrim's Progress* has for its full title *The Pilgrim's Progress from This World to That Which Is to Come* and it traces the journey of Christian from a city which is due to be destroyed by fire, the City of Destruction, to the Celestial City. Carrying a burden on his back, Christian journeys through the Slough of Despond, the Valley of Humiliation, Vanity Fair, and other places where faith and virtue are tested, and encounters on the way various allegorical characters such as Mr. Worldly Wiseman, Faithful, Hopeful, and the Giant Despair. Bunyan's story came to him in a dream. It shows how "the Man that seeks the Everlasting Prize" makes his progress to "the Gate of Glory." A journey to some longed-for haven, undertaken with fervor and solemnity, we call a "pilgrimage." The English Puritans who left Plymouth in the *Mayflower* in 1620 to seek religious freedom and to establish their colony in New England were called "pilgrims" by their governor, William Bradford, and the name "Pilgrim Fathers" was later given to them.

The Christian life is a pilgrimage because it involves making an arduous journey to a chosen destination. The idea of a journey undertaken in the face of great obstacles and in the teeth of fierce enemies has a natural fascination for the human mind. Think of Tolkien's hobbits. In stories such as *The Lord of the Rings* or *Pilgrim's Progress* it is the ultimate purpose of reaching the Cracks of Mount Doom or the Gate of Glory that adds excitement and tension to every struggle over hills or through bogs, across rivers or canyons. This motivation is the key to all the suspense aroused when the traveler lingers in a seemingly delightful place, lured by distractions or trapped by hostile beings.

We think of the opposite of a journey as staying at home, the opposite of movement as paralysis. Few of us like to think of ourselves as standing still. And indeed whatever complaint may be made against modern men and women, surely it is not that there is too little commotion in their lives. Prophets and moralists are always telling us that we rush about too much, here, there, and everywhere. If this is so, how can we expect people to be roused excitedly by the idea of the Christian life as a journey and Christ as the way? A man or woman who commutes daily between home and office fifty miles away does not think of a journey as an exciting adventure. It is a tedious chore. He or she might well say, "I don't want to hear of a God who tells me 'I am your way,' I want to hear of one who says, 'I am your armchair.'"

But mention of the daily hustle and bustle of the commuter reminds us that there is movement which in the long run gets you nowhere. In fact the opposite of a pilgrimage is not necessarily staying at home. It may be moving endlessly without ultimate destination or urgent purpose. If there is neither a ring to be cast into the Cracks of Mount Doom in the land of Mordor nor an Everlasting Prize to be grasped at the Gate of Glory, then movement, however obstructed or delayed, will have neither excitement nor tension: it will not be a pilgrimage.

There is an old classical story about Minos the king of ancient Crete who had a labyrinth constructed, at the center of which he kept the monstrous Minotaur, a creature half-bull, half-man. This beast was fed on seven youths and seven maidens sent annually as tribute from captured Athens. The labyrinth, or maze, was so cunningly constructed that no one who got in could ever find his way out again. It was the young hero Theseus who destroyed the monster. He was aided by Ariadne, Minos' daughter, who fell in love with him. She gave him a thread which he could unwind as he made his way into the center of the maze, and which thus guided him out again.

A labyrinth is an apt symbol for describing movement which gets you nowhere at all. The movement may be feverish, determined, and incessant; but all you do is to keep wandering round, going back on your own tracks, and finding yourself repeatedly in the same place as you were an hour ago, a day ago, or a week ago. This is journeying which leads to no end. It is travel deprived of destination.

It is not surprising that poets have used the maze as a symbol of physical and, more especially, mental activity that is restless but fruitless, movement that may seem for a time like positive progress but always leads up a blind alley. The Scottish poet, Edwin Muir, suffered a great deal of mental stress and anguish and wrote a long poem about his experience which he called "The Labyrinth":

> Haste and delay are equal
> In this one world, for there's no exit, none,
> No place to come to, and you'll end where you are,
> Deep in the centre of the endless maze.

But Muir became a Christian, and after all his experience of the world of mentally going round in circles, meeting himself coming back, and stumbling from one dead end to another, he tells how he escaped the maze, the world of falsehood and error, and tasted the peace of life in the natural world outside it.

There is one limitation about the idea of the Christian life as a pilgrimage and that is that we are tempted to picture God at the destination and to forget that it is he who impels us on our way. Some writers therefore have quite properly presented our course through life as one in which we are pursued by God. We are certainly moving, but we are rather running away from God than towards him. There is a celebrated poem by the Victorian English poet, Francis Thompson, called "The Hound of Heaven," in which God is represented as the divine Hound chasing man, increasingly hot on his heels. The significance of this imagery, as Thompson exploits it, is that it finely expresses our desire not to be "caught" by God, not to be compelled to go after things very different from the various attractions that lure us. It is a poetic device for showing how man wants to set his heart on things below and God wants him to set his heart on things above. The divine will and the human will are in collision. In such circumstances we naturally make a dash for it. And it is interesting that in the very first lines of the poem Thompson uses the image of the labyrinth for the movements the mind makes in trying to evade God.

> I fled Him, down the nights and down the days;
> I fled Him, down the arches of the years;
> I fled Him, down the labyrinthine ways
> Of my own mind . . .

The poet feels that God's pursuit of him is a challenge to many natural inclinations. The call to him to surrender becomes more terrifyingly urgent as the tread of the pursuing feet gets closer and more insistent. It is only at the last, when he finally gives in to his divine pursuer, that he realizes how he has been ignorantly afraid, for in God's hands he will recover all that he has seemingly lost and much more besides. Indeed there is a fine image at the conclusion. The poet has been fleeing from an overshadowing darkness that seemed to threaten his joys and delights. And he suddenly realizes that the darkness which shut out the sun was only the shadow created by God's hand as it stretched out to caress him. The footfall halts on this realization.

Halts by me that footfall:
Is my gloom, after all,
Shade of His hand, outstretched caressingly?
"Ah, fondest, blindest, weakest,
I am He Whom thou seekest!
Thou dravest love from thee, who dravest Me!"

FOURTEEN

Home

THE CHRISTIAN LIFE IS A JOURNEY with a destination, and the destination is "home."

> I looked over Jordan an' what did I see?
> A band of angels coming after me,
> Comin' for to carry me home.

No doubt the meaning of the word *home* for the composer and the early singers of the negro spiritual tugged powerfully at the heart. The "tug" has been exploited in all ages. The words of "Home, sweet home," to Sir Henry Bishop's tune, enchanted audiences for over a hundred years. ("There's no place like home.") It seems that there were those who felt that the appeal of these words could never fail. The *Oxford Companion to Music* unearthed a quotation from an American newspaper of October 1935:

> At Lawton, Oklahoma, John Brett, an attorney, sang *Home Sweet Home* to a jury so as to induce clemency for his client Lloyd Grable, a bank robber.

But it appears, as the *Oxford Companion* observes, that the magic of the song had begun to fade by 1935, for the newspaper report adds: "The jury responded with a verdict of life imprisonment for Mr. Grable." Perhaps the rendering left something to be desired.

Our use of the word *homely* excellently illustrates what the word *home* has come to convey to us. *Homely* can suggest lack of polish or sophistication; but it also suggests friendliness, unaffectedness, warmth, and coziness. Indeed the home is the place, perhaps the one place, where we expect to feel fully at ease, fully relaxed. We are in the presence of those we love, wrapped about with affection and sympathy, secure from physical or emotional coldness, safe from pressures which constrain or inhibit. Small wonder then that we speak of the everlasting life promised us by Christ as life in a "heavenly home."

> Jerusalem my happy home
> Name ever dear to me,
> When shall my labors have an end?
> Thy joys when shall I see?

The lines stress another aspect of the home. It is a place of rest, the place you go to when the day's labors are ended.

> Home is the sailor, home from sea
> And the hunter home from the hill.

Robert Louis Stevenson thus managed to compress into three repetitions of the word *home* a great weight of feeling. Home from sea—from storm and stress, struggle against the elements and the ever-present threat of drowning, home across the vast distances that separate land from land. And home from the hill too—from the wide outer spaces where wild animals are hunted under the chilling night sky.

Heaven is our home; the place all Christians should want to go. But T.S. Eliot observed that "Home is where we start from." Indeed, what else is a home but a place where a baby is born and grows up through childhood to maturity? A home without youngsters can scarcely be said to represent everything that a home stands for. It may well be the place where the elderly put on carpet slippers and sink back into armchairs. But it must also be the place where two-year-olds learn to toddle and three-year-olds learn to talk, where children sometimes make a racket and romp about; not just the place where the old and tired come to find rest, but also the place where the young and vigorous dream dreams and plan projects for the future. For the youngsters home is essentially the place from which they go out into the world.

"Home is where we start from." It is the place of all beginnings as well as the place of all endings. It is where great ventures are conceived, where lifetimes of achievement are foreseen and determined. It is not the place where effort and zeal run down, but where they are wound up. And if our heavenly home is the archetype of all homes, of your home and my home, then nothing ought to be said of the one that does not apply to the other. You praise a commodity of the highest quality by calling it "homemade." You might praise something of the highest quality by calling it "heaven-made." "Home produce" is superior to what is produced outside the home. "Heaven produce" is ultimately what everything that is worth having can justly be called. You are "at home" wherever you are if you feel welcome, relaxed, and secure: the highest praise you can give to a place is to call it "a home away from home." But you are "in heaven" wherever you are if all is peace, joy, and blessedness: all earthly experiences of bliss are "a heaven away from heaven."

There is much in Christian teaching which seems to come "naturally" to human beings. The awareness of a final home beyond the grave is one such truth. Wordsworth pointed to the experience of childhood to indicate that our origin as well as our end lies in an eternal home. The human soul seems to come here from afar and to be not entirely oblivious of its origin:

Not in entire forgetfulness,
And not in utter nakedness,
But trailing clouds of glory do we come
   From God, who is our home:
Heaven lies about us in our infancy!

We come from a heavenly home and the radiance of heaven still hangs about us. Similarly poets in all ages have spoken of the old and the dying as drawing near to their eternal home. When Tennyson pictured the end of his own life and prayed that it might be peaceful, he saw himself setting out to sea and hoped for quiet and tranquillity.

When that which drew from out the boundless deep
   Turns again home.

"Turns again home." The three words strike the ear resoundingly, like a gong, with a sense of utter completeness and finality.

"Show me the way to go home" ran a popular song of the 1920s, and the word *home* can always be relied upon to add a special emotive touch to a lyric. "Home, home on the range..." "There's a little gray home in the west." As the mind lingers among the quotations, a sense of more than earthly peace impinges. When the brothers in Shakespeare's *Cymbeline* bury the body of the young "Fidele," this is how they consign it to the grave:

Fear no more the heat o' the sun
Nor the furious winter rages,
Thou thy wordly task hast done,
Home art gone, and ta'en thy wages.

The job on earth completed, he goes home, taking his wages with him.

Heaven is home, and the Christian has to think of heaven

like that. But this book is not written just to make that point: it is written to make another point too. Heaven is home, and the Christian has to think of home like that. The earthly home ought to mirror the love and fellowship, the joy and warmth, that the heavenly home surely offers. And if any reader wishes to pursue this subject further, he would be well advised to read Thomas Howard's delightful book, *Hallowed Be This House*, which is all about sacralizing the commonplace routines of daily life in the home.

FIFTEEN

House

H OUSE AND HOME." The two words go together. "He
hath eaten me out of house and home": that was the
complaint of the landlady, Mistress Quickly, against her
lodger, Sir John Falstaff, in Shakespeare's *Henry IV, part 2*,
and it has become a common expression. Both words are rich
in emotive associations, but though *home* may have become a
more moving word to English-speaking peoples during the
last two centuries, *house* is the more common and variously
used word in the King James Bible.

In the first place a house is a building in which people dwell.
A church may be called God's house. "Mine house shall be
called an house of prayer for all people." These words from
Isaiah (56:7) were quoted by our Lord himself when he drove
the moneychangers out of the temple. "It is written, My house
shall be called the house of prayer; but ye have made it a den of
thieves" (Mt 21:13). The word is used with a wider application
to a place where God's presence is felt, sometimes without
restriction to a building. After Jacob dreamed his dream at
Bethel, in which God appeared to him and spoke his promises
to him, Jacob said, "Surely the Lord is in this place; and I know
it not . . . this is none other but the house of God" (Gn
28:16-17). Isaiah says "Come ye, and let us go up to the
mountain of the Lord, to the house of the God of Jacob" (Is
2:3), and the psalmist says, "I was glad when they said unto me,

Let us go into the house of the Lord" (Ps 122:1).

Then too, in the Bible and elsewhere, the word *house* is used of the members of the household. "Come thou and all thy house into the ark" (Gn 7:1), God says to Noah. And this usage is extended to cover a family through many generations, so that we speak of the "House of Tudor," and Edgar Allen Poe wrote a celebrated horror story about a doomed lineage, "The Fall of the House of Usher." This is surely one of the most significant usages of the word *house* for Christians; for it enables us to see the "house of God" or the "household of faith," as St. Paul puts it (Gal 6:10), as a related community of people extending through the centuries. "Houses rise and fall," T.S. Eliot wrote, thinking of the way buildings crumble away in time and new buildings have to be made, and also thinking of the way dynasties flourish for a time and then drop into poverty or die out altogether. So it comes naturally to us to think of God's house as a building, or as those who at any given time use the building, or as the continuing family into whose keeping the ancestral home is given. Though the "house" (in the sense of the building) may be destroyed, the "house" (in the sense of the family) may continue to thrive. On the other hand there are circumstances in which even a house (in the sense of a family) may be destroyed, as Poe's House of Usher was destroyed when the last descendant died heirless.

There are other circumstances in which a house cannot survive. Jesus himself said, "And if a house be divided against itself, that house cannot stand" (Mk 3:25). Like a kingdom, a divided household destroys itself. We have other authoritative advice about safeguarding and preserving God's house on earth. It must be wholly grounded in God himself. For the psalmist assures us that "Except the Lord build the house, they labor in vain that build it" (Ps 127:1). We cannot preserve or extend it by our own efforts alone, however strenuous. Then again Isaiah's words "Set thine house in order" (Is 38:1) have entered into the common stock of our expressions for getting things straight or making them shipshape, as we say. "Put your own house in order" is the first thing we say to some meddlesome person who is trying to tell others what they ought to do when in fact he needs to be sorted out himself.

There was a time when men fought duels to the death in defense of what they called the "honor" of their "house," by which they meant the integrity and good name of the family to which they belonged. Macaulay's stirring ballad of how Horatius kept the bridge across the Tiber, the only access to the city of Rome, against invading hordes, begins with a mighty oath from one of the invaders:

> Lars Porsena of Clusium
> By the nine gods he swore
> That the great house of Tarquin
> Should suffer wrong no more.

Of course defending the so-called honor of a house sometimes resulted in cruel and bloody feuds that were carried on for generation after generation. The mutual enmity of the house of Montague and the house of Capulet brought about the deaths of the innocent young couple, Romeo and Juliet. The sense of family solidarity, of the dignity of the lineage, and of the need to preserve something called its "good name" often issued in acts of vengeance and the prologation of hatred and hostility. But it also called out acts of unselfishness, heroism, and self-sacrifice.

Such matters are worth recalling because it may be that we struggle today, in trying to conceive of God's house on earth, against numerous usages of the word *house* that detract from its dignity. In the Bible the word is sometimes endowed with the loftiest and profoundest significance. "For we know that if our earthly house of this tabernacle were dissolved, we have a building of God, an house not made with hands, eternal in the heavens" (2 Cor 5:1). Thus St. Paul speaks. Our bodies are earthly houses which will be dissolved at our death, and we shall enter into possession of a house not made with hands which is eternal in heaven.

We do not spend all our time reading the Bible, however. Perhaps we spend more time reading the newspaper; and in my country "The House rose at 10 o'clock" or "The House was in uproar" conveys information about the nation's government, the House of Lords or the House of Commons. It may not be irrelevant to conceive of God's house in those terms, in that it is at once the authoritative dwelling of lordship and the common home of all people. Or our experience may have colored the word *house* for us through contacts with real-estate agents and their advertisements. In some respects their vocabulary may remind us of what the House of God should be, and in other respects it may remind us of what the House of God should *not* be. It can properly claim to "command a view of the surrounding countryside," we hope, but it can never be "easily maintained" or "trouble-free to run." It can certainly "offer spacious accommodation for a growing family," but it can scarcely be said to "lie in unspoiled surroundings." Nor can the house of God be advertised as either "detached" or "semi-detached," since it must form part of the whole living body and be committed to its welfare. Perhaps, however, it can be said to provide "easy access to all local services." Certainly, as we have already noted, it is fully connected to the main supplies of water and power, for it relies from day to day on the unfailing flow from the reservoirs of divine grace and the powerhouse of divine energy. Moreover it is wired up by telephone to the central exchange where all requests are decoded and whence emergency services are always on call. And it is comprehensively insured against destruction by vandals or enemies through costly premiums paid in blood.

In Britain, we use the expression "public house" when speaking of an inn where refreshment and shelter can be obtained by all who need it, and in this sense God's church is the most public house of all. We speak of a "housekeeper" as one who runs a household, and in a sense all Christians are keepers of God's house. We praise a person who is prudent and thorough in the management of financial resources as being a model of "good housekeeping." Good housekeeping for God must involve the same prudence and thoroughness in utilizing all the resources he puts at our disposal in the world around us. The poets like to call our earthly body a "house of clay," for it is a temporary and ultimately disposable dwelling which is destined to crumble to dust. And indeed our earthly bodies are only "boardinghouses" in that we stay in them for a time only, and they are not our true and final home. Christ's church is the only institution which claims to give us a place in house which we need never leave. It is the only true "house of life." It is the only "housing authority" that offers you more than a building which must ultimately decay. And its "housing policy" is that it offers living space to all who seek it. Unlike the theater, the church never puts up a notice saying, "full house."

Finally, since the church is built upon a rock, it is certainly a lighthouse.

SIXTEEN

Table

WE SAW THAT MEN AND WOMEN inhabiting their human
bodies are in a sense dwelling in "boardinghouses," for
their occupancy of the "house of clay" is a temporary one.
There is a sense, too, in which every church is a "boarding-
house," for Christians gather there to sit at God's board. There
is a verse in a popular hymn often sung at Holy Communion
that runs:

> And so we show thy death, O Lord,
> Till thou again appear,
> And feel, when we approach thy board,
> We have an altar there.

It is one of the most remarkable things in Christian symbolism
that the two things, the table and the altar, should have
become inseparable. After all, the concept of the altar is a
matter of offering up, of giving, of sacrificing. And the
concept of the table is a matter of receiving, of tucking in, of
eating and drinking, of stuffing oneself up with good things.
The full board stands at the center of the hospitable earthly
house as the heart of generosity to others. But it also stands
there as the focus of family fellowship and happiness. When all
is said and done, unless we are ill, we sit down at the table to
enjoy ourselves with those we love and with those we would

befriend. The "groaning board" is a symbol of lavish provision, of warm-hearted liberality. As such, of course, it is a symbol of God's goodness and bounty.

> My table thou hast furnished
> In presence of my foes,
> My head with oil thou dost anoint
> And my cup overflows.

So goes one of the versified versions of the twenty-third Psalm. It is the picture of the loaded table and the overflowing cup which leads the psalmist to add: "Surely goodness and mercy shall follow me all the days of my life: and I will dwell in the house of the Lord for ever" (Ps 23:6). The full table is located in the house of the Lord. So is the altar of offering and sacrifice. The parallel between altar and table is inescapable. So is the parallel between the table in God's house and the table in the family home. The psalmist described the happy man as one whose children should be "like olive plants about thy table" (Ps 128:3). The woman who begged Christ to have pity on her as the mother of a daughter possessed of a devil was reminded that as a Canaanite she was not one of the lost sheep of the House of Israel whom he had been sent to save. "It is not meet to take the children's bread and to cast it to dogs," our Lord said, and the woman's reply was quick and pointed: "Truth, Lord; yet the dogs eat of the crumbs which fall from their master's table" (Mt 15:26-27). Time after time biblical imagery presents us with the picture of men and women nourished by God—and not vaguely and abstractly nourished by God, but given solid food and flowing drink while sitting round a table.

It seems congruous enough with all this imagery that the little ceremony which our Lord ordered his disciples to reenact in memory of his sacrifice should have been a meal around a table, the Last Supper. And it is an interesting conjunction of words in our English Bible that Jesus' act of anger in clearing the temple of sacrilege should have been a matter of overthrowing "the tables of the money-lenders" (Mk 11:15). That is how the King James Bible puts it when Jesus "cast out them that sold and bought in the temple." And he cast out the merchants and bankers because, he said, God's house was a "house of prayer." There was nothing unsuitable, it seems, in the imagery of the house of God as an eating house with full board and overflowing cups. But a shop or a bank where the prime object was to make money, that was a different matter. To be fair, we must notice Christ's accusation: You have turned the place into "a den of thieves" (Mk 11:17). The merchants and bankers were being charged with dishonesty, and we may wonder how our Lord would have reacted if they had been trading honestly in appropriate goods. It so happens that last week I bought half a dozen picture postcards and an illustrated booklet from a little stall at the back of Carlisle cathedral, and I must confess that the dear ladies who were looking after the stall out of the goodness of their hearts and in order to help both tourists and the cathedral funds scarcely looked to me like the kind of people our Lord might have taken a knotted rope to. As for their table of brochures, full of colorful pictures of medieval and later representations of biblical scenes and events, I cannot think our Lord would have been such a philistine as to overturn it. The contrast between the table that belongs in God's house and the table that does not belong is clear enough.

There is another contrast that is worth making. Thanks to the way our language works, we find a curious link between God's table in his house and the stone tables of the law on which the Ten Commandments were inscribed. The law of the old covenant between God and man was laid out on tables of stone. The bread and wine, the body and the blood, of the new covenant between God and man were laid out on a different kind of table. There was a practice in England, and I daresay it is found in America too, belonging to the eighteenth and early nineteenth centuries, of painting the Ten Commandments on boards and putting them up on the walls of churches. I have indeed sometimes seen the Ten Commandments on boards on the east end of a church above or beside the altar. This practice has often been ridiculed. Somehow devotions are not aided when, lifting up one's eyes from the pew, one stares at the words "Thou shalt not covet thy neighbor's wife." Quite apart from the uncovetable character of most neighbors' wives, the stark reminder of the law expressed in negatives standing there above the table from which one would receive the sacrament of love seems incongruous. One is reminded of the young lady who protested that she found the Ten Commandments unhelpful. "They don't tell you what to do," she complained, "and they put ideas into your head." Reflecting on the matter now, however, I can see a point in being confronted by the tables of the old covenant displayed behind and above the table of the new covenant. The contrast is sharp. The one is a matter of numbered regulations laid out in sequence like a society's rules and conditions of members. The other is that table at which one is asked to be God's guest. We may fitly recall George Herbert's words again.

"You must sit down," says Love, "and taste My meat."
So I did sit and eat.

It is interesting that a thing so handy and ordinary as a table can acquire associations of great grandeur and dignity. Think what noble associations gather round the words "Round Table" because of the ideals and exploits of King Arthur and his knights. Then, by contrast, compare the expression "card table" in which the word *table* sheds its dignity and awesomeness. As I look around my study I wonder what other items of furniture have names that can acquire comparable richness. Certainly a chair can. We speak of a "Chair of Philosophy" at a venerated university and great dignity accrues to the term *chair*. But there are other items of furniture that do not seem to lend themselves to being upgraded or glamorized, say drawers or shelves. What prevents us from taking these articles by name into the language of poetry or worship? "O Lord, thou hast stocked my shelves with the cans of thy bounty and packed my drawers with silk and polyester."

C.S. Lewis made an old wardrobe a gateway to the magical country of Narnia. The homeliest items of furniture are capable of being transfigured. It was George Herbert again who observed that a servant who sweeps a room with God's cause in her heart not only makes the room "fine" and clean but makes the act of sweeping a "fine" act too. The lowliest and most humdrum objects and acts acquire richness when used or done in God's service. In short, the fact that a word like *table* can be pedestrian in flavor or grand in flavor is not just a fact of language but a fact of life. In exploring how words work, we explore what life is all about. A lot has been made of the fact that Jesus chose common things like bread and wine to be received as his own body and blood. I think more ought to be made of the fact that Jesus took one of the most unromantic, one of the crudest things we do and made it the medium of his self-offering to us. I mean eating and drinking. No one who thinks seriously about what goes on in the mouth and throat and stomach when we eat or drink can deny that these processes are the reverse of exalted or romantic. They are activities that we share with dogs and monkeys, cows and rats. Yet done at God's table, they are the means of carrying out his most sacred command. The teeth that chew the hamburger close on the bread of heaven, the throat that swallows the soft drink is moistened by the wine of life.

Recently I heard Alistair Cooke remark on the radio that in England when a bill is "tabled" in the House of Commons, it is brought up for discussion, but that in America when a bill is "tabled" in Congress, it is shelved. I could not help thinking how two aspects of God's table are present in this distinction. We put the bread and wine on the table in order to feed on them (to "discuss" them, as a nineteenth-century writer might have said); but we put them on the table too in order to have done with them ourselves and to offer them up to God.

Then yesterday morning I went to St. John's Church, Keswick, and the parish priest preached about St. Mary Magdalene. He noted how our Lord was sitting at table when Mary came and anointed him with precious oil. "She turned the table into an altar," he said. That, I suppose, is what we ought to do every time we have a meal by saying grace.

SEVENTEEN

Milk

O NE OF THE MEMORABLE BIBLICAL IMAGES of God's bounty
to us is represented by the words "milk and honey." The
Israelites were promised "a land flowing with milk and honey"
(Ex 3:8). The words suggested a lavish provision of what is
delightful to consume and rich in nourishment. They keep
their meaning for many of us. But, then, I belong to the
generation that was brought up by nutritionists who recom-
mended people who needed to be built up in health to
consume milk and butter, eggs and cream, cheese and honey,
and the like. Such commodities are no longer in fashion
among health experts. Animal fats now have the bad name
which, thirty years ago, carbohydrates had, and potatoes now
have the good name which, thirty years ago, proteins had.
Perhaps we shall soon get an updated Bible in which God
promises his people "a land well-stocked with fibers and
vitamins." Be that as it may, for centuries the associations of
"milk and honey" have been rich and tasty. The words bring to
mind fields full of lowing cattle and carpeted with lush, moist
grass and the air alive with the hum of bees moving from
flower to flower in the sunshine. They suggest, not just a
well-stocked larder and an appetizing meal on the table, but
also a luscious countryside well watered yet bright and
abundant.

But of course what is significant about milk is that it is

99

something more than a symbol of a well-stocked table and a flourishing farm life. There is human milk as well as animal milk to reckon with. Milk flows in the fruitful household from mother to baby. The baby at the breast is the symbol of tranquil, flourishing home life. As for honey, I do not know how modern advertising techniques work in this respect, but I remember being told by an experienced artist and writer some thirty years ago that among the sure-fire pictures to put on the jacket of a new book about nature or gardening was a beehive and bees. "It will always sell a book," he said. We all know the comparable imaginative and emotional pull exercised by a picture of a baby being suckled. Back in the 1930s, when Mussolini was anxious to strengthen his image as a tough, masculine boss of a richly fruitful, family-conscious, yet well-ordered nation, he had himself photographed on a visit to a maternity hospital at feeding time. Long rows of beds were occupied by mothers, each with a baby at her breast, and all holding them in identical positions. Surveying this scene stood the mighty dictator, the chief engineer, as it were, of this disciplined Italian fecundity, looking as lordly as if he had fathered the whole wardful.

There is small need for an Englishman to remind Americans of the rich associative power of the word *honey,* for American men have taken it as their chief word of endearment for American women. (And it is odd that this particular Americanism has never been imported into Britain.) Certainly writers in all ages have used it as the supreme term for sweetness—"sweeter also than the honey and the honeycomb"; and even today I notice that American health enthusiasts are more likely to call their girlfriends "Honey" than "Fiber." In some of the most hauntingly lavish lines in English poetry, Coleridge's *Kubla Khan*, the poet pictures a state of ecstatic intoxication:

For he on honey-dew hath fed,
And drunk the milk of Paradise.

In *Macbeth,* Shakespeare used the expression "the milk of human kindness," and the connection between milk and human kindness has seemed so natural that the expression has come into common use. Shakespeare also spoke of the "milk of concord."

The way the baby draws nourishment from the mother's breast illustrates the total dependence of the offspring upon its mother, which is snapped only when the child is weaned. This physical dependence of the child upon its mother, generation after generation, shows the human race linked together by a chain of dependence reaching back to Eve. James Joyce toyed half-seriously, half-comically, with that other physical linkage between offspring and mother, the umbilical cord. This is a surer linkage than that of breast-feeding. Many babies have been nourished by bottle-feeding and thus missed one link with their mothers, but no babies have been born without umbilical cords. Joyce pictured the whole human race linked together by umbilical cords, all eventually stretching back to Eve. The linkage he compared to a telephone system. We are all wired up to the central exchange which is Eve's belly. (Joyce even plays with the notion of putting a call through, right across the system, right through the centuries, to Edenville 001.) Some people may find the analogy distasteful, but it vividly represents the interconnectedness of the human family through the ages.

When we have dwelt upon the nourishing content of milk and its way of flowing through the bodies of mother to children in all ages, it is appropriate to turn to the New Testament use of the image. "As newborn babes, desire the sincere milk of the word, that ye may grow thereby," Peter says (1 Pt 2:2). The milk of the word is the truth of the gospel in a form that the least mature persons can assimilate, but it is essential to growth. "I have fed you with milk, and not with meat," Paul says in the same vein (1 Cor 3:2). In each case the image is of mother's milk that nourishes the baby before it is able to digest meat. Thus, handing on the word is the most natural of processes in the continuity of family life. You either provide the nourishment of the word, or you do not provide it. None of the epistles instructs us to deny the young child the word until it is old enough to digest meat. Neither Peter nor Paul wrote, "Do not speak of God's truths to people until they are able to understand them fully and to make up their own minds about whether they have need of this kind of teaching or not." Failing to convey the truths of the gospel to people is like denying the breast or the bottle to a baby, the result of which is death. Not speaking is starving.

The "milk of the word" may be an early diet to prepare people for the meat of the word. But the milk must not be watered down. Talk of watering down mild is one of the most common expressions for dilution that take the real quality of a thing away.

Things are seldom what they seem.
Skim milk masquerades as cream.

So goes a song in Gilbert's *H.M.S. Pinafore*. The expression we use for divesting something of its worthwhile substance is "milking" it. You "milk" a business if you draw on its capital and deny it investment.

The two most frequently portrayed representations of Christ are as the crucified Savior on the cross and the baby in his mother's arms. Artists have pictured the child at his mother's breast in such a way as to bring out the human reality of the divine incarnation and to surround the child with emotive associations of innocence, tenderness, and love. Sometimes the Christ child has his mouth to the Virgin's breast. In such cases one ought to be able to sense the process of nourishment at work. For the flow of milk is the active reality, the movement of life to life, hidden in the static grouping of mother and child.

EIGHTEEN

Debt

WE HAVE SPOKEN OF GOD'S BOUNTY in nourishing us. We have fancied ourselves as guests at his table. We have savored the taste of milk and honey and pictured the Savior of the world at his mother's breast. We are in danger, an austere critic might say, of wallowing in sentimentality, of presenting the Christian message in a picture-postcard format complete with color photograph and mellifluous verse. So let us not forget another very different theme that runs through the Bible. We are not always represented as God's favored children and the recipients of his bounty. We are also represented as his debtors. "Forgive us our debts, as we forgive our debtors," goes the Lord's own prayer (Mt 6:12). And debts were treated very seriously in New Testament days. In our Lord's parable of the unforgiving servant whose own debts were forgiven by the king and who then proceeded to extort his due from fellow servants, we get a clear picture of current practice. The fellow servant begs for time. The unforgiving servant rebuffs him and casts him into prison until the debt is paid.

Debts and indebtedness are indeed a serious matter. They raise sharper issues, more precise matters, than are raised by comforting talk about the furnished table and the overflowing cup. Jesus himself did not hesitate, it seems, to use the language of the marketplace and the bank. The "Son of Man," he said, "came to give his life a ransom for many." And St. Paul took up the image. "For there is one God, and one mediator between God and man, the man Christ Jesus; Who gave himself a ransom for all" (1 Tm 2:5-6). We are familiar with ransom demands these days. They are a favorite device used by terrorist organizations. We are equally familiar with the phenomenon of debt. But we don't usually connect it with God. We watch the mounting figures on the monthly statement from MasterCard or Visa with apprehension, but it seems remote from the emotions involved in our relationship to God. It is a different kind of problem. We may take out our calculator to help solve it, but not our prayerbook.

Yet John Donne preached a fine sermon before King James I at Whitehall in February 1625 in which the language of the marketplace takes on new meanings. We complain about the poor price one gets for land these days, he says. But wasn't it always very cheap indeed? How cheaply did Adam sell the Garden of Eden—a highly desirable estate, if ever there was one? How cheaply did he sell the human race? What price did he ask in selling immortality? Donne reminds his congregation what the sale of eternity amounted to. What is the value of a country manor, of a county, of a kingdom, or of the whole world, compared to what we sell when we trade our souls, our consciences, our future immortality, in exchange for a few grains of earthly dust which is all that we can possess here? We decry a man who sells a town or an army to the enemy; but Adam sold the whole world and its inhabitants—including Abraham and Isaac, Peter and Paul, evanglists and apostles: they were all sold by Adam. For Adam sold the whole race in advance. The whole race. He even sold the Virgin Mary herself. Indeed, had not Christ been sinlessly conceived, he too would have been bartered away in advance.

This image of the human race, sold into captivity under sin, clearly appealed to Donne's ingenious imagination. He presses the image even further elsewhere. He pictures the sinner who has sold himself into the hands of the Devil by his taste for earthly possessions and lustful indulgences, and warns how the Devil will falsify the accounts further against his victims when they are sick and near to death by simply adding zeros to the existing figures of the debit account. He warns his congregation not to think they can get away with it as the pirate gets away with it by coming back to settle at home with his ill-gotten gains and bribing his way to a pardon. You can't do that, Donne tells his listeners. You may try to do it—by endowing a hospital or leaving your money to a good cause—but God cannot be bribed like that.

We all know that human indebtedness is not always a financial matter. "I never could repay him," we say of someone who has done us a much-needed good turn. You may think you are heavily indebted to the mortgage company or bank that lent you the cash to buy your house. But you know that you are, strictly speaking, more heavily indebted still to the fellow who grabbed you from behind just as you were stepping off the pavement in front of a bus. As for the donor who came to your family's rescue when your daughter urgently needed a bone transplant to save her life, how do you measure your indebtedness to him? Or to the surgeon who performed the operation? And what about that teacher of whom you say, "I shall be eternally grateful for what he taught me," or that father or mother of whom you say, "I could never thank them enough?" A network of mutual indebtedness links the human race together. It is no less real than the physical networks of flowing milk and severed navel-cords that join the human family in one.

Donne's imagery of Adam's thriftlessness in selling the human race and of our own thriftlessness in selling ourselves into sin is not the same, you may say, as imagery which defines us as so heavily indebted that Christ's self-sacrifice alone can ransom us. In the one case we sell our birthright extravagantly; in the other case we buy selfish pleasures extravagantly. But of course buying and selling are the same process. In either case you trade something for something else, money for goods, or goods for money. And whether the money you receive is totally incommensurate with the goods you part with or the goods you receive are totally incommensurate with the money you part with makes no difference.

The indebtedness of the human race to God is something like what we call a "national debt." What a bewildering expression that was to us when we first heard it as children! What a revelation of life it was when a schoolteacher first tried to explain it to us. How does it work? As far as I can understand it, rather like this: A government wants to spend fifty million dollars on a battleship. It hasn't got the fifty million dollars in the bank. So it prints pieces of paper called "savings bonds" and sells them to its citizens. Thousands of citizens buy thousands of these bonds at a hundred dollars each. Why do I buy some of these? Because the government will pay me twelve dollars per year for each one I have bought. It will stop paying me only when I sell the share to someone else and he starts to collect the annual interest, or when I sell it back to the government at the end of the term. How can a government afford to pay twelve dollars a year for borrowing a hundred dollars that it will have to pay back? Strictly speaking, it can't. But when one set of bonds has run its term and the government has to buy them back, it can always fund the purchase by selling more bonds to someone else. Provided most of the purchasers prefer to collect their twelve dollars a year rather than to cash in their bonds, there can never be a moment of truth. If all the lenders of money by the purchase of bonds in any country decided to unload their bonds, the system would collapse. Thus the system is sustained on an ever-increasing indebtedness. What it all amounts to is that the community as a whole is massively in debt, is forever increasing that debt, and only pays off a bit of the debt by incurring a new debt. And if this is not a description of the relationship of the human race to God, I don't know what is. When we, as we like to think, "do something for God," by putting more in the church collection plate, by contributing to the new organ fund, or by supporting the work of Christian missions and Christian efforts for the poor and handicapped, the most we can flatter ourselves with is that we have borrowed a bit more from God in order to express our gratitude to him tangibly. And of course earthly parents know a good deal about this game. It is one of your pleasures as a father or mother to buy your own birthday present, concealing the exact nature of the process as far as you can, so that little Johnny really does think he has done something for you in putting down cash for a box of handkerchiefs—cash that he obtained from you first. It is his grateful "thank you," and he has slightly increased his indebtedness to you by being so generously grateful. The question, "Who bought the handkerchiefs?" must not be pressed, as a matter of courtesy. And God, of course, is all for courtesy himself.

In the world of finance we can see human communities sustained only by piling mountain upon mountain of indebtedness. In the world of the family we can see children accumulating ever greater loads of indebtedness. We all owe debts to others that we can never repay. In the personal, as well as in the national financial sphere, human insolvency is universal. No wonder the image of the Savior is that of one whose ransom price clears off all debts.

NINETEEN

Inheritance

T HERE IS ANOTHER THEME in Christian teaching which has
financial overtones. It is the theme embodied in such
words as *heir, inheritance,* and *testament.* St. Paul spells it out
very clearly that "we are children of God; and if children, then
heirs; heirs of God, and joint-heirs with Christ" (Rom 8:16-
17). It is generally a man's children, his sons and daughters,
who inherit his estate. We, of course, are not God's children in
the same sense that Christ is God's Son. We are not God's
begotten sons and daughters. We are, rather, "adopted"
children. By being adopted we become "joint-heirs" with
God's only-begotten son, Jesus Christ. Being redeemed involves being adopted.

The word *heir* works in an interesting way. You hear of a very
rich oil magnate and you ask "Who is his heir?" meaning "Who
will inherit his estate?" Notice that you are right to ask, "Who
is his heir?" and need not ask, "Who *will be* his heir?" In other
words we define a person as an heir on the strength of what is
coming to him in the future. At first sight you might be
tempted to argue that it would be more accurate to say, "John
will be his father's heir" than to say, "John is his father's heir."
But would it? For as soon as John has inherited the estate, he
ceases to be the heir to the estate and becomes the owner of the
estate. Someone else is now the heir; John's own son, if he has
one.

I can speak of the girl to whom I am engaged to be married as "my future wife" or "my wife-to-be"; but we do not speak of a rich man's son as his "future heir" or "heir-to-be." We speak of him as the heir. And when we get down to more precise detail the same usage applies. The Prince of Wales is Queen Elizabeth's "heir apparent," which means that so long as he survives, his right to succeed is incontestable. But when George VI came to the throne in 1936, Princess Elizabeth, the eldest of his two daughters, was not "heir apparent" but "heir presumptive"; which means that as things stood she would have an incontestable right to succeed to the throne, but if perchance she acquired a baby brother, he would by law replace her, becoming "heir apparent." Now whether a person is "heir apparent" or "heir presumptive" is not necessarily a matter of sex. A childless king might have his younger brother as "heir presumptive," but that brother would lose his status if the king acquired either a son or a daughter.

This rigmarole is introduced in order to stress that an heir is an heir *before* he inherits. Whether heir apparent or heir presumptive, an heir ceases to be an heir as soon as he becomes king or succeeds to an estate. It would be impossible to be an heir to a throne which you already sat on or to an estate already in your possession.

John Donne puts the matter simply in one of his sermons when he insists that we are "heirs of heaven," "heirs of the joys of heaven," "heirs of the glory of heaven." These are clearly things whose possession lies in the future. And it is something of which we need to be constantly reminded in this vale of tears, that we are heirs of joy. It is something of which we need to be constantly reminded in this often drab, somber, and even depressing life, that we are heirs of glory. Donne, as we might expect, is not content to leave the matter there without bringing his ingenuity to bear on it further. He develops the notion of heirdom in an illuminating way. He distinguishes between two contrasting kinds of heirdom; the one called *gavel-kind,* and the other called *primogeniture. Gavel-kind* defined a system of inheriting by which all the children of the deceased shared his estate equally between them. *Primogeniture* defined the system of inheriting by which the eldest son inherited the entire estate. Now the remarkable thing about our succession as heirs of heaven, Donne says, is that it is not gavel-kind inheritance on a shared-out basis which leaves one heir looking over his shoulder at what another heir has got. Neither is it the usual principle of primogeniture which leaves one son with everything and the rest enviously in need. Rather it is a unique form of primogeniture for all, for everyone gets everything he could possibly want.

One cannot talk about heirs and inheritance without talking about wills or testaments. The word *will* in the most obvious sense is simply an inclination or intention. My will is my determination to do this or that. He is "strong-willed," we say, of someone who insists against odds on getting his intentions carried out: At least we say he is "strong-willed" if we admire what he is doing. Otherwise we say he is "stubborn" or "obstinate." A cynic once conjugated what he called an "irregular verb" to cover this variation of usage. It goes:

I am strong-willed
You are obstinate
He is pig-headed

However that may be, a person's "will" in the first place is his intention, and when that intention is applied to the disposal of his property after death and is formally written down on paper and signed, it becomes his "will" in a more tangible sense.

The main distinguishing feature of a "will" in the latter sense is that it is something which becomes effective only after the death of the person whose "will" it is. God, like many human beings, has made two wills, Donne tells us in one of his poems. The first will was inscribed on tablets of stone. They held the Ten Commandments, the old law, which impossible for men and women to obey in every detail without lapse. God's second will, which bequeathed his kingdom to his heirs and became effective on the death of Christ, abridged the clauses of the earlier will into the command that we should love God and one another. Thus the old will or "testament" was superseded by the new will or "testament."

In our day-to-day life most of us, I trust, spend very little time speculating whether we are heirs to this or that person's estate. Our parents probably told us exactly how they intended to dispose of their property between our brothers and sisters and ourselves. Nevertheless there must still be many cases where men or women die without having direct descendants or obvious heirs. Similarly many men and women have or acquire obligations to others than their own children. So when the deceased has been committed to the grave and the family mourners have gathered in the lawyer's office, there may still be a good deal of uncertainty and apprehension among those who watch the unfolding of the will and listen intently as the lawyer reads it aloud.

Has Father remembered Aunt Susan, struggling on her meager pension? Has he rewarded the housekeeper who nursed him through his last failing years? Has he treated his early orphaned nephew as virtually one of his own children? Has he left something to his parish church or to his favorite charity? I know of a somewhat eccentric businessman of considerable wealth who died recently. When all the interested parties gathered to hear how kindly they had been remembered, they were aghast to learn that every penny of his estate had been left to homes for dogs and cats. The approach of death had not softened him toward his nearest and dearest nor, it seems, toward the human race in general.

We believe that there can be no last-minute discovery about what the will of God is. We may question individually what right we have to be treated as heirs, to be adopted into fellowsonship with Christ. But whatever cause God may have to be justifiably angry with us, the biblical promise gives us reason to trust that there will be no final surprise revealing that heaven is to be exclusively populated by cats and dogs.

TWENTY

Hands

I HAVE JUST LOOKED UP THE WORD *hand* in a Bible concordance. I found so much space devoted to it that I decided to make a few quick comparisons. I found that *hand* and *hands* (not to mention *handful, handmaid,* and so on) had over twice as much space as *head* and *heads* or *face* or *body* or *blood.* In fact, if you want to find words with more space devoted to them than *hand* or *hands,* you have to turn to such words as *God, Jesus, good,* and (very interestingly) *fear.* It seems to me that we learn something about the Christian faith when we discover that a Bible concordance gives more space to *hand* and *hands* than to *heart* or *mind* or *soul.* Because this does not seem to be typical of literature in general. When I looked up *hand* and *heart* and *soul* in a general dictionary of quotations, I found far more quotations under *heart* and *soul* than under *hand.*

The Christian emphasis on hands is illuminating. Consider the functions of hands. What do they do? They work of course. They make things. They are the main physical instruments of human action. True, what they do is determined by the mind and the will that direct and control them. We must not exalt physical activity without reference to its aim and purpose. A bulldozer can shift in an hour a quantity of earth which it might take twenty men a day to move by hand. But the man who operates the bulldozer is using his brain to guide his hands; otherwise it would not do anything useful at all. And the bulldozer itself is a product of the human brain's inventiveness.

When all is said, *hands* make us think of action as surely as *mind* makes us think of thought. But the mention of a hand does not usually conjure up notions of crude activity, as, for instance, the word *fists* does. "He used his fists to make his point" conveys that someone has been striking out aggressively. "He had to resort to his fists" implies a fight. We do not, on the whole, use the word *hands* when thinking of crude toil. We don't say, "This is a delicate task that requires a lot of thought, but that is a matter of crude handwork." Instead we say, "This is a delicate task that requires a lot of thought, but that is a matter of crude spadework." Digging becomes "spadework," while the words *handwork* and *handicraft* are used for the skilled and delicate operations that produce fine lace, fine pottery, fine carving, and the like. Digging a garden may be "spadework," but making a fine tapestry is "handwork." We may refer to the elbow when we want to speak of crude toil but not to the hand. We value an artifact more highly if it is "hand made" or "hand woven" than if it is manufactured by a sophisticated machine.

The explanation of this usage, I suppose, lies in the sheer sensitivity of the hands. I once read an account of a monk who had to deal with the griefs and distresses of men and women in a troubled part of the world where privation and persecution were the order of the day. He was a man of warm human feelings, deeply stirred in his sympathies. Women would come to him in deep distress and burst into tears upon his shoulder. It was observed that he had developed a technique of giving them maximum physical support and emotional comfort without bringing any intrusive and unhelpful element of personal sexual tenderness into the situation. He would throw his arm comfortingly around the woman's body but all the pressure terminated at the wrist, from where the hand was flung back at right angles to the body.

I tell this story simply in order to illustrate the sensitivity of the human hand. The hand may be contrasted to the head in terms of physical activity as opposed to mental activity, but never in terms of crude activity as opposed to refined or sensitive activity. That is why we can speak of being "in God's hands" to reassure ourselves. Because the business of caring, protecting, and loving so often involves use of the hands. We speak of giving a person "a helping hand." We think of the "healing hands" of a surgeon, the "gentle hands" of a nurse, the "open hand" of a benefactor. Remember the degree of trust and friendliness involved in saying "Here is my hand" and contrast it with what is implied in saying, "Here is my foot" (or "my boot!") or "Here is my fist." Lovers go "hand in hand." The young man seeks the girl's "hand" in marriage, and the ceremony in physical terms revolves around the placing of a ring on a finger. Think what associations of warmth and intimacy, trust and love, are contained in the simple requests, "Join hands," or "Give me your hand."

It is the hands that our language treats as the instruments of giving help ("Lend me a hand"), providing resources ("I had everything at his hands") and even nourishment. For the worst thing you can say of people's ingratitude is that they "bite the hand that fed them." To sign a document is to give your hand to it. Somehow the hand has become the symbol of commitment for the body as a whole. Hence the custom of shaking hands in friendship, in greeting, or in making a compact. Somehow the hand can represent the body at full stretch in love or generosity, in care or even in sway. For we say, "The hand that rocks the cradle rules the world."

Of course the word *hand* is not always used with generous, affectionate, or positive associations. We speak of tyrants ruling "with an iron hand." We characterize sinister conspiratorial machinations as "the hidden hand" at work. The murderous act is the "hand of Cain." But it should be noted that, whereas expressions such as "Join hands" or "I give you my hand" rely wholly on the emotive power of the word *hand* itself, the negative expressions derive their pejorative force from additional words such as "iron" or "of Cain."

It is small wonder that powerful associations cluster around the use of the word *hand* or *hands* both in the Old Testament and in the New Testament and also in Christian prayer and teaching throughout the ages. Think of the psalmist's words:

> For he shall give his angels charge over thee,
>   to keep thee in all thy ways.
> They shall bear thee up on their hands,
>   lest thou dash thy foot against a stone. (Ps 91:11)

Or think of those other words of the psalmist which have become a part of public and private worship: "Into thy hands I commend my spirit" (Ps 31:5). Jesus himself quoted them from the cross at the last: "Father, into thy hands I commend my spirit"(Lk 23:46).

There are numerous references in the Bible to the hand of God, the right hand of God, and the good hand of God. Many such references call up notions of power and glory. "And ye shall see the Son of man sitting on the right hand of power," Jesus said boldly and majestically to the high priest (Mt 26:64). And the phrase "at the right hand of God" (or "of the Father") runs through Christian liturgies. But there are many biblical references too which call up notions of intimate loving care and protectiveness. "My sheep hear my voice, and I know them, and they follow me; And I give unto them eternal life; and they shall never perish, neither shall any man pluck them out of my hand" (Jn 10:28-29).

Hands can be laid on people in a hostile or a comforting manner. In our Lord's parable of the unforgiving servant, he tells how the man went and found one of his fellow servants who owed him money and "laid hands on him and took him by the throat," demanding payment of the debt (Mt 18:28). But the biblical associations with the laying on of hands are generally of a very different kind. When the apostles chose new leaders they first prayed and then "laid their hands on them"

(Acts 6:6), and when Peter and John went down to Samaria to confirm new believers in the faith, "then they laid their hands on them, and they received the Holy Ghost" (Acts 8:15). In the long history of the church since then, hands have been laid upon people's heads in ordaining, consecrating, confirming, and healing.

In this context one should remember the two-way traffic of the spirit through the hands. Human hands are laid on men and women to transmit strengthening, healing, or consecrating power from God to his children. But human hands are stretched in prayer, transmitting our requests to God. Indeed the image of hands outstretched in prayer is common to the Bible and to all literature which touches either human yearning for God or the yearning of men, women, and children for each other.

If we want to set any matter or any person at a distance from us, detaching ourselves from deep personal concern with it or with them, we "wash our hands" of the issue or the individual, as Pilate did. But if we want to impress someone with the thought that something is going to impinge on their lives with immediacy and urgency, then, like the prophet of old, we say, "The day of the Lord is at hand" (Jl 1:15). And if we want to stress the personal closeness of God's help and comfort we say, like St. Paul, "The Lord is at hand" (Phil 4:5).

The gruesome business of crucifixion involves driving nails through hands and feet. We have referred already to T.S. Eliot's image of Christ as the surgeon who operates on us, though he is himself wounded. We lie in the operating room, our own wounds probed by the bleeding hands of the healer. It was because Pilate washed his hands clean that Christ's hands were covered with blood. This may be the cost of washing one's hands of other people and their concerns.

TWENTY-ONE

Potter and Clay

"I N THE HAND OF THE LORD there is a cup, and the wine is red," the psalmist said (Ps 75:8). There is a fascinatingly relevant image in Isaiah: "But now, O Lord, thou art our father; we are the clay, and thou our potter; and we are all the work of thy hand" (Is 64:8). There are various contexts in which writers have spoken of human beings as clay. Shakespeare speaks in one of his sonnets of the time when he will be mixed with clay, meaning the time when he will be dead and buried. Here clay is associated with lifelessness. Indeed clay is often an image of fleshly mortality. Dryden speaks of a living human being as one who inhabits a "tenement of clay." Here we are on earth for a time in lodgings made of clay. In a petulant mood Byron wishes he were "so much clay" instead of being a creature of blood and bone, passion and feeling. Clay, for him, is lifelessness and insensitivity. There is a passage in Daniel (2:31-32) about an image with a head of gold, breast and arms of silver, belly and thighs of brass, whose feet were "part of iron and part of clay." Its weakness lies in its feet, which are easily broken in pieces. The saying, "Your idol has feet of clay" has come into our language to describe someone whose underlying weakness or deficiency renders his apparent superiority hollow and unreal.

Imagery therefore which speaks of men and women as being clay in the hands of the divine potter emphasizes our lack of strength and substance, and our essential lifelessness, until we are taken in hand and and molded into something useful, something with its own shape and purpose. It also emphasizes our comparative worthlessness as raw humanity. In Shakespeare's *Antony and Cleopatra,* when Antony wants to assure Cleopatra of his overwhelming love for her, by comparison with which his power as one of the rulers of the Roman empire is nothing, he exclaims, "Kingdoms are clay!" They are negligible. They count for nothing by comparison with Cleopatra. So to label men and women as clay is to point out the arrogance and absurdity of human beings when they presume to question their Maker. Isaiah asks: "Woe unto him that striveth with his Maker. . . . Shall the clay say to him that fashioned it, What makest thou?" (Is 45:9). And St. Paul takes up the same image in the Epistle to the Romans (9:20): the "potter has power over the clay," he tells us, to make what he wants of it, and it is ridiculous therefore for the thing which has been made to turn on God and ask, "Why have you made me like this?"

This image of the divine potter and the human potter is not peculiar to Christianity. In the *Rubaiyat of Omar Khayyam* there is a fable in which the poet stands in an old potter's shop, surrounded by rows of earthen vessels. Some of them can speak and some cannot. One who can asks the question: "Who is the Potter, pray, and who the Pot?" The question evokes a brief discussion among the pots. One pot fears that he has been taken from the earth and cunningly shaped only to be stamped back into the earth in the long run. Another replies that only a bad-tempered being would fondly make a bowl, enjoy drinking from it, and then destroy it in anger. After a silence, an ugly, ill-made vessel complains that it has been so long neglected that its clay has gone dry. But "fill me with the old familiar juice," it says, and perhaps I might recover.

The notion that we are first clay and then vessels in the hands of a divine Potter is clearly a long-established one that is rich in meaning and lends itself to fruitful development. Robert

Browning took up the image in his poem, "Rabbi ben Ezra," in which the Rabbi muses on the coming of old age and, out of the wisdom of his years, gives advice to his young disciples. At the end of the poem he turns to the metaphor of the potter's wheel. It is the wheel of time and change on which we lie like passive clay. The rapid movement of time, the whirl of history, the spinning away of present into past, are simply the operation of the machinery on which we are molded. The grooves left near the base of the vessel in our earlier days may be decorated with more delightful designs than the comparatively grim things worked around the rim in our later days. But what matters is the use of the cup. In climax Browning pictures a "festal board" where lamps glow, trumpets peal, and new wine foams as the Master lifts the cup to his lips. This is the ultimate purpose of our experience here. The wheel of time and experience spins dizzily beneath us, but our business is not to fasten our eyes downwards on the machinery on which we are molded. It is to look upwards and foresee our function in slaking the thirst of the divine Creator.

The image of human beings as vessels in the hands of the divine Potter reminds us of the sheer brittleness of humanity in the hands of God. When the psalmist wishes to express God's power over erring men, this is the image he chooses. "Thou shalt dash them in pieces like a potter's vessel" (Ps 2:9). If one seeks a moral to be drawn from the image of ourselves as earthenware vessels, surely it is here. No artifact can be more useful than a simple cup to a race of beings utterly dependent from day to day upon liquid refreshment. No artifact can be more useful and precious than a finely wrought vessel. Yet nothing can be more easily destroyed. One careless movement of the hand and the vessel is shattered in fragments. In one of his marriage sermons John Donne fancied himself, before God took him in hand, not as an earthenware vessel, but as the earth from which the Potter might make a vessel if he chose, and, having made it, might break it too if he chose. He then went on to an image drawn from the minting and use of coins.

At a time when the king's face was stamped on all coinage, this was a useful parallel. Christ is for all time the image of the Father, "the same stamp upon the same metal." But in what sense am I an image of the Father? Donne asks. He sees himself as an old coin which had its Maker's image imprinted on it at its creation, but it has been so worn, defaced, and ground away by many many sins that it is now no more than a "piece of rusty copper."

There is one other aspect of clay which enriches the image of the human being in the hands of the divine Potter. Clay may be heavy, doughlike, shapeless stuff, but it is above all malleable. You can pick it up and do something with it. It does not resist like iron or stone, which require the tools of the blacksmith and the sculptor if anything is to be made of them. There is no question of hammering or chiseling. Tools do not intervene between the maker and his medium. True he needs his spinning wheel, but his hands work directly on the clay. So susceptible is the clay to being shaped that when we criticize someone for being too easily influenced by another, we say, "He is like clay in her hands." The phrase suggests the surrender of the individual will in devotion and obedience.

First we are clay in God's hands. Then we are earthenware vessels into which the treasure of God's grace is meant to be poured. Without this content the vessel remains empty; though, as we know, the empty vessel makes the biggest noise.

TWENTY-TWO

Garden

E ARTHENWARE VESSELS: they make me think of plant pots—
peculiarly useful for their proper function of keeping
growing plants alive and utterly useless for almost every other
purpose by reason of the hole in the bottom. When you look
around for a container in which to scoop up some water and
your eye lights on a row of plant pots, you know you'll have to
seek elsewhere. The plant pot is designed to keep its contents
enclosed on all sides yet exposed to the sky above and to the
earth beneath. It is a miniature garden.

Gardening is one of the favorite hobbies of Englishmen,
perhaps *the* favorite hobby. Like books on diet, touring, and
do-it-yourself activities, books on gardening line our book-
shop shelves. There is a popular magazine called *Homes and
Gardens* which manages in its title to combine the emotive tug
of two of the most emotion-packed words the Englishman has.
I am not typical in this respect. I have never enjoyed gardening.
Perhaps I am too impatient. You can spend a week decorating a
room and three weeks later you can sit in it and enjoy the fruits
of your labor. But if you spend a week pruning and weeding a
garden, then three weeks later you will find that the job has to
be done all over again.

Gardens have to be constantly tended, and very laboriously
too. But it seems that the first garden of all, the Garden of

Eden in which the biblical story begins, did not at first impose arduous toil on its inhabitants. In Milton's *Paradise Lost* the Garden of Eden is described as being "a heaven on earth," for it contains the whole wealth of nature within its compass. Nevertheless it takes a certain amount of looking after. Indeed it is Adam's great delight to observe that he and Eve will have to produce a good few "younger hands" if they are going to keep up with the needful prunings. It is however a place of sheer joy. Adam and Eve together do just enough gardening to make them appreciate a subsequent rest and to give them a healthy appetite. They exist in an idealized setting where, even when reclining on the ground, they have only to stretch out a hand to take a fruit from a nearby bough, and it comes away effortlessly in their hands as they grasp it. They recline together on a bank of flowers, which they find soft and downy. When you recollect that they are naked, you realize how idealized this picture is. In the gardens of our experience, surely we could not lie down in the nude without finding ourselves soon covered with scratches and bites. But no, Adam and Eve lie comfortably there with lions, bears, and tigers romping cheerfully around them, and even the elephant providing good-humoured entertainment by doing amusing gymnastics with its trunk. Adam and Eve even chew the insides out of oranges and use the empty skins as cups, and all, apparently, without the need to interrupt their fondling of each other, which surely, in the fallen world we know, would be a very sticky business indeed. Thus the garden is the place of all perfection and delight. Essentially it is the home of innocence. For what could be more innocent than bears that gambol and elephants that perform party tricks? And what could be more innocent than the first woman's first sight of her own face mirrored in a stream? It smiles back at her delightedly and, *not yet knowing that it is herself she is looking at*, she smiles appreciatively. When she meets Adam for the first time a few moments later she thinks him less beautiful than that face in the stream. Quite so. She judges simply on appearances, with no vanity to interfere. This is a true revelation of the character of innocence. So is Eve's subsequent decision, made only after yielding to Adam in love, that in him there is after all a "manly grace and wisdom" that shift the balance of preference.

For Milton the earth is the image of heaven, as hell is the perversion of heaven. Men and women are images of God, as Satan is a mock-up parody of God. The Garden of Eden represents what the earth was meant to be when God created it, just as Adam and Eve represent what men and women were meant to be when God created them. There is a traditional symbolism that represents woman as man's garden, the very body of his world in which he delights, and which brings forth fruit from the seed he plants. Love poetry has for many centuries toyed with imagery of this kind. We find it in the Song of Solomon. "A garden inclosed is my sister, my spouse; a spring shut up, a fountain sealed" (4:12). This image of the enclosed garden and the sealed fountain has a rich history in subsequent literature. *Hortus conclusus, fons signatus* ("enclosed garden, sealed fountain"): these words define a theme many poets have turned to. They should be recalled when we come to deal with the word *bride*.

In English life gardens can readily become a source of amusement, as anyone who has ever lived in a rural village knows. Many a village will have its annual show at which the produce of local husbandry is displayed. There is enthusiastic competition to win prizes awarded for the the largest tomato or the largest cucumber. The triumphs tend to have a statistical, rather than a nutritive, value. Gardens lend themselves to sentimentalization too. There is a much-quoted verse which runs:

The kiss of the sun for pardon,
The song of the birds for mirth,
One is nearer God's heart in a garden,
Than anywhere else on earth.

The mellifluous lines slip too smoothly through the mind. After all, the story which began in the paradisal Garden of Eden reached its climax in the Garden of Gethsemane and the Garden of the Resurrection. It seems appropriate that Christ's agony, like Adam's first sin, should have been set in a garden. It is even more appropriate that the sepulchre in which Christ was buried should have been in a garden and the first meeting of Mary Magdalene with the risen Christ in the garden too.

Adam has been called the first gardener. There is a very old riddle that runs:

> When Adam delved and Eve span
> Who was then the gentleman?

It implies that human beings had their jobs to do from the beginning of creation and that the invention of a class called "gentlemen," who did not have to work for a living, was a development of much later history and a development not anticipated by God. One of the gravediggers in Shakespeare's *Hamlet* tells us that "gardeners, ditchers, and grave-makers" all belong to "Adam's profession." This recognition of Adam as a gardener makes all the more moving St. Mary Magdalene's mistake when she has seen the empty tomb and first notices Jesus standing before her. She assumes that he is the gardener. And, of course, as the second Adam, in a sense he is.

Thomas Campion, an Elizabethan doctor and a skilled lyricist, wrote a celebrated song that begins "There is a garden in her face." It suggests the flowerlike beauty of the girl's complexion and features, the white and red of her brow and cheeks and lips, the rich fruitfulness of her smile. It would not be inappropriate to observe that a suitable theme for meditation on Christ himself might be: There is a garden in his face. There are three gardens in fact; the Garden of Eden, the Garden of Gethsemane, and the Garden of the Resurrection. The facial lineaments bear forever marks of the events of the three gardens of the fall, the agony, and the rising.

TWENTY-THREE

Face

T HE FACE IS THE PART of the human body which most surely reveals character and mood. It is essentially the part of our bodies which is to be looked at. We should think anyone odd who insisted on talking to us with his eyes on our feet. We should judge him lacking in confidence. Or if we lack confidence ourselves, we should wonder whether our shoelaces were undone or we had accidentally put on socks from two different pairs. To be able to look a person in the face is to be fairly and squarely on genuine, honest terms with that person. The face is our showpiece to the world. We inspect it in the mirror every morning to check up that it is in a condition to be looked at. A new pimple or disfigurement worries us more than a disfigurement anywhere else. I read yesterday of a woman who had to have a section of her face—her left cheek and eye—removed for cancer. Plastic surgery can happily do wonders these days, and you would not have known from her photograph that any such treatment had taken place. Nevertheless the emotional consequences of her experience were such that she desperately needed companionship of a kind which could fully sympathize—companionship with others who had undergone the same operation. So she advertised for contacts, determined to form links between fellow-sufferers who had had cancers removed from their faces.

We have only to read a few lines about cancer of the face to react inwardly in a peculiarly sharp and intimate way. We hear of cancer of the lung or of the stomach, and we are touched by a sense of distress and even of fear for ourselves. But when we hear of cancer of the face the shock is not necessarily more painful, but somehow closer and more intimate. A tingle comes to our own cheek. There is an instinctive tendency to raise our hand to our own face, "Oh, not that!" we think. "Anything but that!" Thus to slap someone's face is the worst possible insult, except perhaps to spit in someone's face. Yet St. Matthew tells us how the Jews spat in Christ's face and punched him and slapped him (26:67). Reading of these events and picturing them stirs a more personal sense of shame than even reading of the pierced hands and bleeding side.

There would be no point in stressing how often the words *face* and *eyes* occur in the Bible, because of course they recur frequently in any literature which touches movingly on human experience. But in view of the closeness and intimacy which references to the face and the eyes so often evoke, it is noteworthy that there is so much biblical use of the words *face* and *eyes* in reference to God himself. An event achieves a new dimension for us as soon as it is said to have been done "before the face of the Lord." The phrase brings God into the picture with a personal immediacy that is inescapable. The Jews prayed, and people have continued to pray, for God to turn his face away from their sins. The face-to-face encounter with God is the summit of human experience. It was granted to Moses: "And the Lord spake with Moses face to face, as a man speaketh unto his friend" (Ex 33:11). And the psalmist declared: "When thou saidst, Seek ye my face; my heart said unto thee, Thy face, Lord, will I seek" (Ps 27:8).

How else can intimacies between God and man be recorded? How else can God be conceived at all? For indeed a "faceless" God is inconceivable. We use the word in disgust and disapproval of people who operate in a sinister and unfeeling or irresponsible way behind closed doors—"faceless bureaucrats" or "faceless secret police." There is a story told of Oscar

Wilde that, being encountered in the street one day by a journalist he knew who had written unflatteringly of him in print, and determined to cut him to the quick, he refused his proffered hand and said, "I'm sorry. I recall your name very well, but I'm afraid I can't remember your face." When we want to suggest that some business or institution has redeeming qualities, we say, "It has a human face." The phrase probably derives from a poem by William Blake from his collection *Songs of Innocence*. It is a simple, touching poem called "The Divine Image":

> For Mercy, Pity, Peace, and Love
> Is God, our father dear,
> And Mercy, Pity, Peace, and Love
> Is Man, his child and care.
>
> For Mercy has a human heart,
> Pity a human face,
> And Love, the human form divine,
> And Peace, the human dress.
>
> Thus every man, of every clime,
> That prays in his distress,
> Prays to the human form divine,
> Love, Mercy, Pity, Peace.

No wonder it is promised that in heaven God's servants "shall see his face" (Rev 22:4). On earth the virtues have a human face, a human body, and a human dress. But these are aspects of the "human form divine," for all virtues in their essence are "God, our Father dear."

When we use the word *face* metaphorically, it is often out of a desire to suggest openness and stillness. The phrase "the face of the earth" somehow conjures up a picture of stretched-out terrain that is open to the sky. And we condemn offences against openness and candor as "two-faced." There are few condemnations in our judgment of fellow beings more scornful than to declare them "two-faced." Yet I suppose it would be only in praise of someone that you might call him "four-handed" or "four-footed." You might call a dexterous juggler "four-handed" or a fast runner seemingly "four-footed." A person who has "eyes all over his head" is a person who seems to miss nothing at all. And you say, "I am all ears," when you are prepared to listen attentively to what someone has to tell you. It appears that eyes and ears, hands and feet, can be multiplied flatteringly; but you cannot duplicate the face without a suggestion of duplicity. In this respect the face is like the mind, the heart, and the tongue. "A double-minded man is unstable in all in ways," St. James says (Jas 1:8). The psalmist declares how the flatterer speaks with "a double heart" (Ps 12:2). And St. Paul says that deacons must not be "double-tongued" (1 Tm 3:8). It is fascinating that if I say, "He bore that day more than you would think a single back could bear," you would think sympathetically and admiringly of the man. But if I suggested that he conveyed more than you would expect a single face to express, you would take it as a criticism of duplicity.

The association of the face with openness and singleness of purpose is close. To "face" something is to put all pretense and self-deception aside. Thus you "face" the consequences when you come clean over an issue. When you decide to own up frankly to some mistake you have committed, you decide to "face the music." When your courage fails and you feel incapable of dealing with a crunch that might ensue from your coming clean, you say, "I can't face it." So far as word-usage is concerned, evil in respect of the eyes is lust or covetousness, evil in respect of the heart is envy and anger; but evil in respect of the face tends to be deception and dissembling. I do not mean that we cannot speak of an "angry face" or a "cruel face" or a "lecherous face" but that the face is the part of the body we should first turn to for images of deception precisely because the honest face is the symbol of candor and truthfulness. "God has given you one face and you make yourself another," Hamlet says to Ophelia when he wants to be offensive to her on the subject of the way women use cosmetics.

It has been a theme of Christian literature that to see the face of God is more than a human being can endure. In Newman's *Dream of Gerontius* the dying Gerontius dreams that his soul is led after death by an angel through regions where eventually he passes within earshot of the devils in hell and later within earshot of the angels in heaven. Indeed the angels are singing the celebrated hymn, "Praise to the Holiest in the Height." Shortly afterwards Gerontius is brought into the presence of God. But he is there for only a fraction of a second. In the magnificent musical setting of this by Elgar, the moment of glimpsing God's face is unforgettable. It is approached by an urgently escalating crescendo that culminates in a crash like a bombshell, and all that is heard immediately afterwards is the voice of Gerontius shrieking in top register, "Take me away!" The merest glimpse of the divine face is intolerable to the unpurified human soul. Conversely the loss of that vision is in another way intolerable. In Marlowe's play, *Dr. Faustus*, in which Faustus sells his soul to the Devil, Mephistophilis, in exchange for a lifetime in which diabolical powers are at his disposal, there is an episode where Faustus questions Mephistophilis. Where are you damned? he asks. In hell, Mephistophilis replies. Then why are you out of hell here and now? Faustus persists. And in a sudden irresistable passion Mephistophilis forgets himself. This is hell, he says. I'm in it all the time. Don't you realize that anyone who has once seen God's face and tasted heaven's joys lives in a permanent hell, a permanent torment, when he has lost that bliss? For a moment, under the impact of thinking about heaven, even the Devil has to admit publicly the misery of damnation:

Why this is hell, nor am I out of it.
Think'st thou that I, who saw the face of God,

And tasted the eternal joys of heaven,
Am not tormented with ten thousand hells
In being deprived of everlasting bliss?

In the same play when Faustus sees a vision of Helen of Troy, whose unrivaled beauty caused the rivalry that sparked off the long siege of Troy by the Greeks, he exclaims: "Was this the face that launched a thousand ships?" Indeed its beauty sent the Greek fleet across the sea and provoked a ten-year struggle that has been celebrated in European literature ever since. So powerful is the image of the human face in literature. The image of the divine face, immeasurably more powerful still, has magnificence and grandeur superimposed. The most eloquent and emotive of all spoken blessings is surely the one Moses had from God himself:

> The Lord bless thee, and keep thee. The Lord make his face to shine upon thee, and be gracious unto thee. The Lord lift up his countenance upon thee and give thee peace.
>
> (Nm 6:24-26)

TWENTY-FOUR

Eyes

THERE IS AN OLD STORY of a little girl who had a teddy bear which she called "Gladly." And when her mother asked her why she had chosen such an odd name for him, she said, "Because he's cross-eyed." The mother was still mystified until the little girl reminded her of a line in one of her favorite hymns: "Gladly my cross I'd bear." The pun is a clever one and, though the joke is well-worn, I retell it now because it seems to me that there is a sense in which Jesus himself must have been "cross-eyed," in that clear marks of the suffering he was to endure must have been readable in his look. And it follows that we too ought in that sense to be "cross-eyed." For the eye is the most expressive part of the human face and ought to carry some kind of reminder of the saving cross. Indeed since the cross is at the heart of Christian thought and action, we have good reason to extend the pun and say that what we are about from day to day ought to be "cross-fertilized"—fertilized by the saving cross. For that matter our mental approach to the troubles of other people needs to be "cross-grained." Moreover our motives ought to be "cross-purposes," and our reflections ought to be "cross-references." Paradoxically, the Christian way is a "cross-road," and the Christian must make his progress through life "cross-wise." Indeed we shall evade our Christian vocation unless our enquiries into Christian duty and Christian truth are a series of "cross-questionings."

To consummate our puns, the great mystery at the heart of human life is nothing less than a cosmic "cross-Word puzzle."

Yes, there are indeed more ways than one of being "cross-eyed." To that extent the little girl stumbled unconsciously on a revealing insight.

> The light of the body is the eye: if therefore thine eye be single, thy whole body shall be full of light. But if thine eye be evil, thy whole body shall be full of darkness.
>
> (Mt 6:22-23)

Jesus' words give the eyes priority and centrality in the body, for the eyes light up the whole. If the human body is God's house, then indeed it is a lighthouse. "Keep me as the apple of thine eye," the psalmist prayed (Ps 17:8). The "apple" is the pupil, the central, most crucial, most cherished part of the eye, which is itself perhaps the most cherished part of the body. For if you want to suggest that something is more desirable to you than anything in the world, you say, "I'd give my eyes for that." To give one's eyes is the ultimate sacrifice (short of giving one's life). No price could be higher, and nothing more valuable than what is worth such a price. If there is any part of your body that you protect with especial concern, it is your eyes. They close instinctively at the sound of an explosion, of splintering glass, or falling shrapnel. Your hand rises instinctively to cover them. The psalmist knew that he was asking the utmost in terms of loving protection when he asked to be looked after by God as preciously as a person would look after his own eyes.

Literature is full of references to the eyes as the source of light and loveliness, and there are many references which associate the beauty of heaven with the beauty of human eyes. "Paradise stood formed in her eyes," says Chaucer of his entrancing heroine, Cressida. "Grace was in all her steps, heaven in her eye," says Milton in describing unfallen Eve. What a concentrated tribute that is; grace in every step, heaven in the eye—surely it sums up the essence of living in innocence, living in unbroken communion with God; to make every step taken an act of grace and to carry the light and love of heaven in the eye.

The eyes both give and seek. They shed light and love, and they beseech light and love. Even a dog's eyes, when they stare at you, seem to be asking as well as giving. Cats' eyes, on the other hand, give less away and express detachment rather than dependence. Cats see well in the dark. We call the glass studs on our roads which sparkle in our headlights "cats' eyes." They are a great boon to motorists. Human eyes seek the "cats' eyes" and are rewarded by guidance.

"I will lift up mine eye unto the hills, from whence cometh my help," the psalmist says (Ps 121:1). The lifting up of the eyes to God in worship and prayer is prior to any shedding of light or love upon fellow human beings. The theme of lifting up human eyes to God runs alongside the theme that God's eyes are looking down on his people. "For his eyes are upon the ways of man, and he seeth all his goings" (Jb 34:21). The mutuality is important. The interchange of sympathy from eye to eye in the relationship between man and God is what makes possible the interchange of sympathy from eye to eye in relationships between people.

We have just lived here through two weeks of heavy cloud, drab gray skies, and chilling pre-spring winds. Lifting up the eyes to the hills and sky has been for some weeks a ready recipe for bringing a weight of gloom upon the spirits. At least that's how I see it. The locals, born and bred here, have a degree of resignation in these matters which makes them seemingly impervious to the gloom. Unless the rain or the sleet is pelting down in bucketfuls, they will say, "It's a nice day," when you greet them. This attitude tends to make one feel guilty about one's less enthusiastic response to the leaden skies, but after all it appears that the Roman legionaries regarded a tour of duty up here, guarding the Roman wall against the Scots, in much the same light as a Muscovite soldier might look upon a transfer to Siberia. Anyway it seems to me that if gray skies don't depress you a bit, sunshine will scarcely give you an exciting lift by contrast. I make this point because this morning the sun is shining for the first time in two weeks, and if I lift up mine eyes to the hills I see that the mountaintops are capped with snow that is gleaming white against the blue sky. It is therefore much easier today to think in terms of a benevolent God's eyes shining down upon his people than it was yesterday. The question therefore comes to mind: Is the human scene such that we should expect God's eyes to be shining down brightly on it from day to day? What should we think of a God who was capable of such indifference to the brutality and misery that he surveys?

In all ages the kindness of God has been described in terms of sunshine and his anger in terms of cloud.

> Though thou with clouds of anger do disguise
> Thy face; yet through that mask I know those eyes,
> Which, though they turn away sometimes,
> They never will despise.

The eyes of God may turn away from the human scene as cloud obscures the sun. The averting of the divine eyes may be in hurt, disgust, or even anger at what is to be seen below. But it will never be in scorn. God will never despise his people. That is how John Donne read the variations of the weather.

We read God's divine nature in what he has made. And reflecting on the eyes and the eyesight he has given us, and how they respond to the world he has made, we come up against the same paradox that we encountered in thinking about fire and water and so many other things he has made. You cannot have a fire that warms comfortingly without a fire that burns painfully. As with touch, so with sight. The inspiringly beautiful snow-capped peaks around her, now dazzling white under a blue sky, and a sheer delight to the eye, have claimed the lives of five young climbers in the last few weeks. That is one kind of contrast. But a more immediate and inescapable contrast for the eyes in a region such as this is the contrast between the sense of glowering divine disfavor cast upon the earthly scene by heavy, iron-gray cloud, and the cheering sense of divine loving-kindness implicit in the lighting up of field and road, farm and cottage, by the glow of sunshine. If the eye is the light of the body, the sun is the light of the earth.

It requires an act of faith to sustain the view, through days and weeks of grayness and gloom, that the basic reality of creation is not thus most accurately represented to the human eye. The belief that sunshine is a surer symbol of reality is faith. Anyone is at liberty to come along and declare that such belief is wishful thinking. He might record the hours of sunshine per year and the hours of cloud and establish statistically that grayness is the norm. Just so a pessimist has no difficulty at all in establishing that disappointment, frustration, and pain form so large a proportion of human experience that the notion of a loving God and a benevolently created universe is absurd, and the notion that the human race has reason to be grateful for existence is laughable. Confuting the pessimist involves an act of faith. But it is not an act of faith that closes its eyes to evil, misery, and suffering, or pretends that they are not so bad after all. The cloudy days *are* gloomy. The proportion of misery is an almost overwhelming fact of life. All thinking Christians respond to William Cowper's words that "God moves in a mysterious way," stirring up the sea, riding on the storm, covering the sky with cloud. But Cowper reminds us that clouds which we dread may carry a load of divine mercies that will rain down upon us in blessings.

Judge not the Lord by feeble sense
But trust him for his grace;
Behind a frowning providence,
He hides a smiling face.

All imagery of Christ as the light of the world is imagery that appeals to us as creatures with eyes. The connection between eyes and light is so crucial that either word would be meaningless in a world where the other did not exist. The proclamation at creation, "Let there be light!" would be nonsense if there were neither eyes nor eyesight. Though perhaps it would be more instructive to note that eyes and eyesight would be of no avail in a world without light. For it is probably easier for us to conceive of men and women like ourselves trying to grope their way about a world of darkness, than to conceive of a race of eyeless beings in a visible world. The image of Christ as the light, "the true light that lighteth every man that cometh into the world" (Jn 1:9), enables us to grasp what existence in a world of darkness might mean. Richard Crashaw wrote a delightful "Hymn of the Nativity," sung supposedly by the shepherds who visited the manger in Bethlehem:

> Gloomy night embraced the place
> Where the noble infant lay:
> The babe looked up, and showed his face;
> In spite of darkness it was day.
> It was Thy day, sweet, and did rise,
> Not from the East, but from Thy eyes.

Thus at Bethlehem the blessing which God instructed Moses to use, and which was quoted at the end of the previous chapter, was fulfilled in a new and amazing way. The Lord made his face to shine upon us in the flesh.

TWENTY-FIVE

Veil

THE NOTION OF A CLOUD that hangs over human heads and hides God's brightness from our eyes has a rich history in literature. Cowper's idea that the cloud is a frown behind which God's smiling face is concealed and Donne's suggestion that the cloud overhead is God's anger with human sinfulness that masks his loving eyes both present the cloud in a wholly negative way. It conceals the brightness of God's kindness and mercy. The cloud symbolizes what for the present cuts us off from the fullness of God's light and love. A great medieval mystic of the fourteenth century wrote a treatise called *The Cloud of Unknowing*. It is a study of contemplative prayer and it develops the theme that the cloud of unknowing which cuts us off from knowledge of God cannot be penetrated by the human brain but only by "a sharp dart of love." Again the cloud is seen as an obstacle to men and women in their relationship with God. But we may recall that Francis Thompson, in his poem *The Hound of Heaven*, eventually realized that what had seemed like a cloud overhead proved in reality to be the shadow created by a protective hand stretched over him. The cloud may be seen as a threat; or it may be seen as protection.

There is no doubt that when the sun blazes down with its full power on human beings, they have to run for shelter. The shade of a roof, a tree, a parasol, or a Texan hat is needed to keep off blinding summer sunlight, to save us from sunstroke.

There are parts of the equatorial world where exposure to sunlight could soon kill. In such a context the idea of a cloud as a protective shield is more likely to occur to the mind than the idea of a cloud as an obstacle. There is no special reason to picture the light of God's blazing love as a watery gleam in the pale sky of a climatically temperate country where men and women are hungry for warmth and dearly long to see the clouds swept away from before the face of the sun. On the contrary there is every reason to picture the light of God's blazing love as white-hot fire whose touch on the naked skin would scorch till it smoldered.

No Christian can doubt that, however strong our faith, however ardent our prayers and devotions, here on earth we are cut off from face-to-face confrontation with God's glory and even from sustained heart-to-heart awareness of God's boundless love. However open saints and mystics have been to God's touch, and however vividly they may have sensed his presence at moments of rapture or of crisis, they all remind us that day-to-day life involves passing through periods of spiritual dryness when faith has to do its work without any warming awareness of the sunshine of God's love.

When T.S. Eliot recorded a rapturous momentary glimpse of paradisal light and joy at the beginning of his *Four Quartets*, he did so with an account of an experience in a Gloucestershire garden that occurred when he was looking down into a dry concrete pool that had been drained of water. A sudden burst of sunlight above seemingly flooded the pool with a glittering light. "Then a cloud passed, and the pool was empty." The message which came to the poet then, seemingly through the voice of a bird, was that "human kind / Cannot bear very much reality." Indeed, we creatures of earth could no more endure the revealing of God's brightness, the unveiling of his face, than we could endure the full glare of tropical sunshine or the flash of a nuclear explosion. The cloud that veils God's brightness is a merciful shield.

There is a sobering corollary to all this. We are protected not only from the brightness of heaven whose dazzle would burn and blind us; we are protected also from the glare of hell which would sear and shrivel us like the advent of a second Hiroshima.

St. Paul speaks of God, the King of kings and Lord of lords "dwelling in the light which no man can approach unto" (1 Tm 6:16). When Moses was called up into the mountain to receive the tablets of stone, we are told, a cloud covered the mountain, "And the glory of the Lord abode upon Mount Sinai, and the cloud covered it six days: and the seventh day he called unto Moses out of the midst of the cloud. And the sight of the glory of the Lord was like devouring fire on the top of the mount in the eyes of the children of Israel" (Ex 24:16-17). Later God permitted Moses the sight of his "back parts" only because to see his face would be fatal. "Thou canst not see my face: for there shall no man see me and live" (Ex 33:20). In Isaiah's great vision of heaven even the seraphim cover their faces with two of their six wings (Is 6:2). The poet Edmund Spenser, in his "Hymn of Heavenly Beauty," portrays the glory of the divine majesty whose "least resplendent spark" makes the sun and moon dark by comparison. He advises us to prostrate ourselves and not to dare to look up with our corruptible eyes on the face of God—

> For fear, lest if he chance to look on thee,
> Thou turn to nought.

Other poets have pictured God in a light of such intensity that blinded eyes could see nothing. In this sense the light has the practical effect of darkness. "Dark with excessive bright thy skirts appear," Milton wrote in a picture of God enthroned in heaven. While another seventeenth-century poet, Henry Vaughan, wrote:

> There is in God (some say)
> A deep but dazzling darkness

These are attempts by poets to summon up in the mind a sense
of light so overwhelmingly bright that the contrast between
brightness and darkness is lost in sheer dazzle.

The fact that Christ is the light of the world encouraged
poets in the past to make playful comparisons between the Son
of God and the sun. John Donne has an Eastertide poem on the
Resurrection in which he urges the "old Sun" to sleep a little
longer and recover from the wound it received by the
darkening of the sky on Good Friday. The world can put up
with it if you dally and take a rest, he tells the "old Sun." "A
better Sun rose before thee today." And later, in a hymn to
God written in his last sickness, Donne prayed to God that at
his death God's Son should shine as he has always done.

I draw attention to this pun because T.S. Eliot gave it a new
lease of life in his *Four Quartets*. We have already noted his line
about the end of the rapturous visionary moment, "Then a
cloud passed, and the pool was empty." The theme of a cloud
passing before the sun runs throughout his poem. "The black
cloud carries the sun away," is a crucial line in which "sun" can
be read as "Son." The pun is a fruitful one. Not only was there
darkness over all the land on Christ's death on the cross, but a
cloud carried the Son away on the mount of Transfiguration,
and a cloud carried the Son away at the Ascension.

If we had imaginations washed through and through by the
baptismal waters of regeneration, perhaps we should not be
able to watch a cloud carry the sun away without reflecting on
the great biblical theme of light and darkness. We would
"read" the sky as reflectively as we read a poem, searching for
half-hidden meanings, the glimpses of the true nature of
things that can be caught in the workings of the natural world.
The cloud above is the cloud of unknowing that only love of
God can penetrate; it is the frown of providence which hides
God's smiling face; it is the sign of divine anger with sin that is
the other side of the coin of God's love for us; it is the shadow
of God's caressingly overreaching hand; it is the shade
that protects us from the intolerable brightness of God's face;

it is a small version of that total eclipse that accompanied Christ's death on the cross. And it is also the cloud that veiled him from the disciples at the Transfiguration and at the Ascension.

The Israelites recognized that some kind of partition must stand between the most sacred things and the doings of the workaday world. Such a notion does not necessarily imply that the doings of the workaday world are outside the realm of what can be sanctified. On the contrary, the partition exists because the source of all sanctification must be protected in its full intensity from the casual approach, the thoughtless touch, the irreverent glance. So, at the heart of the temple, the Holy of Holies into which only the priest could enter was partitioned off by a double veil. It was this veil that was torn from top to bottom at the crucifixion.

The veil, then, is what protects the sacred from profane touch. The fact that Christ's death on the cross blew the distinction sky-high is logical. What act could have been more destructively profane than that which took place under the connivance of the High Priest that day? It was the ultimate desecration.

What have we to do with "veiling" in our lives today? In a sense all human clothing is veiling; it carries away from daily sight bodies that might otherwise excite to rapture or lust. When Eve is first portrayed in Milton's *Paradise Lost,* she wears her hair trailing like a veil down to her waist. When the angel Raphael appears before Adam in the Garden of Eden, he stands "veiled with his gorgeous wings." And when Satan approaches Eve to tempt her, he sees her "veiled in a cloud of fragrance." Indeed, such is the veiling required for natural beauty as for the ultimate Beauty. If natural human beauty seems thus to be such that it must be veiled from hourly sight in the workaday world, if something called "reverence" seems to be called out by human beauty, then it is not to be wondered at that the face of God and the deep mysteries of God must be veiled from human scrutiny.

TWENTY-SIX

Tongue/Voice

T HERE IS A CURIOUS EXPRESSION which we use when we want to stuff a home-truth down someone else's throat and tell them to swallow it. We say, "You can put that in your pipe and smoke it." I don't know whether the expression is American or British in origin. It sounds as though it might be Indian. Be that as it may, the Irish have an even more colorful way of conveying the same conviction. They say, "You can set that to music and sing it."

The Israelites were continually setting to music and singing the praise of God, his holy name, his wondrous works, his might, and his power. Throughout the history of the Christian church human voices have been lifted up in worship and prayer wherever the faith has spread. The mouth is opened to carry man's prayer to God; and the mouth is opened to carry God's message to man. When the Holy Spirit descended upon the apostles at Pentecost tongues of fire appeared over their heads, and shortly afterwards their new-found inspiration burst forth in a miraculous gift of utterance—the "gift of tongues."

The voice of God delivered the law to Moses (Ex 20). To Job (37:4) and to the psalmist (18:13) the voice is the voice of thunder. Indeed for the psalmist it is "powerful" and "full of majesty," it breaks cedar trees and sets the earth shaking. But to Elijah, of course, God spoke neither in the wind, the earthquake, nor the fire, but in a "still small voice" (1 Kgs

19:12). In the New Testament God's voice is heard at Christ's baptism (Mt 3:17) and at the Transfiguration (Mt 17:5), in each case declaring Christ "my beloved Son, in whom I am well pleased." It is heard again by the disciples as the days of the passion approached (Jn 12:28-29). Conversely the psalmist speaks of crying unto the Lord with his voice (3:4), and prays that his voice will be heard (141:1). Man's duty is the dual one of listening to the voice of God and voicing God's praise and his own supplications.

The power of the tongue for good or ill is made very clear in the Bible. St. James has a lot to say about its power for ill. It is a little member but is capable of great damage. The evil tongue defiles the whole body. Its fire is the fire of hell (Jas 3:6). What gives special force to this image is that the tongues which lighted above the heads of the apostles blazed with the fire of heaven. The duality in the image of fire is what we should expect. For Isaiah God's anger fills his lips with indignation and makes "his tongue as a devouring fire" (Is 30:27). The notion of the tongue as a flaming fire-raiser is not confined to apostolic blessing by the Holy Spirit. "Death and life are in the power of the tongue," we are told in Proverbs (18:21). It is the instrument of heaven or of hell. And it is a sharp and forceful instrument. "They bend their tongue like their bow for lies," Jeremiah says of the wicked (9:3), and a moment later, "Their tongue is as an arrow shot out" (9:8). Again later in Jeremiah (18:18) we find "come, and let us smite him with the tongue." We are apt to think of the tongue as a flexible member whose evil is done by subtle insinuation. But here the tongue has the tautness of a bow, the deadly swiftness of an arrow, and the hardness of a sword. Neither tautness, swiftness, nor hardness need be at the service of evil, however. The member which became the symbol of apostolic power had need of all these, and other qualities. "Though I speak with the tongues of men and angels," St. Paul begins his celebrated exhortation to charity (1 Cor 13:1), conceiving the tongue as the instrument of rich golden rhetoric.

The power of the tongue for good or ill is not a matter of dispute. We have all heard many a sermon warning us of the dangers of loose talking, idle gossip, and tale-bearing. Such warnings have no doubt been repeated in every century in the history of the Christian church. But in our own century the power of the tongue has been immeasurably increased. Think of the voices that were about the ears of an average country-man of a hundred years ago. He heard the voices of his family, his friends, his workmates, his boss, and if he were a church-goer, the voice of his parish priest or minister, offering up prayers and proclaiming the word of God. And think of the voices that are about his ears today from the radio and the television. The dissemination of the spoken word has now surpassed the dissemination of the written word, for there are many more who can and will listen than there are who can or will read. Our little picture of the villager of a hundred years back reminds us that the invention of printing spread new "voices" about our countries. Bibles were read in country churches and country cottages. Classics found their way into village schools. Newspapers percolated into every little hamlet. Indeed it was confidently proclaimed that the pen is mightier than the sword.

But the printed word is silent unless you pick up a book and read it. The spoken word is vocal whether you hear it or not. The psalmist may have said, "My tongue is the pen of a ready writer" (Ps 45:1), but he might just as significantly have said, "My pen is the tongue of a ready speaker." Printed pages are pickled speech. Books are no noiser as they stand on the shelves than are phonograph records as they stand in their racks. It is not books and records, strictly speaking, that are about our ears—unless we choose to open and read, to put the disc on the turntable and switch it on. It is voices that are about our ears. We may not have the most comfortable civilization of all time; we may not have the most cultured civilization of all time; we may not have the most prosperous civilization of all time; but we certainly have the noisiest civilization of all time.

Even in remote rural areas planes zoom overhead and trucks roar past garden gates. And everywhere radio and television assault our ears with news, advertisements, chat, drama, and sheer aimless flippancy.

Let us dwell mentally for a time on the vivid Biblical imagery of the tongue, whether the tongue is used in praise or in malignity. Let us dwell on the rich positive usages of the word *mouth*: "for the mouth of the Lord hath spoken it" (Is 40:5).... "Out of the mouths of babes and sucklings" (Ps 8:2) ... "My mouth shall show forth thy praise" (Ps 51:15).... "then was our mouth filled with laughter" (Ps 126:2). Then let us note the powerful negative usages of the word *mouth*: "Violence covereth the mouth of the wicked" (Prv 10:6).... "a flattering mouth worketh ruin" (Prv 10:6). And let us dwell too on the exalted usages of the word *voice*: "the voice of the Lord is full of majesty" (Ps 29:4).... "his voice was like a noise of many waters" (Ez 43:2) ... "the voice of one crying in the wilderness" (Jn 1:23). Somehow all these usages seem to take us into a world where what is said matters, where silence is the norm rather than utterance. They do not seem to belong to an environment that is as laden with noise as is our own. I say "laden" because it seems to me that the sheer weight of noise and the incessancy of utterance weigh heavily on the human spirit. "Be not afraid," says Prospero in Shakespeare's *The Tempest*, "the island is full of noises." In Elizabethan days it was still apparently a positive thing to say that the place was full of noises. Clearly the noises were not our noises. One thinks of singing birds, humming bees, and clicking crickets. But we have a world so full of noise that neither humming bee nor clicking cricket is likely to be audible. Indeed I suggest that the environment which Prospero described as "full of noises" is one which would have provoked you or me to say, "How beautifully quiet it is!" The sounds of nature were not drowned by the drone of planes, cars, lawnmowers, and spin-driers. When the Irish poet, W.B. Yeats, stopped in his tracks one day to stand on the gray London pavement amid the bustling traffic and to dream of the lake isle of Innisfree in his far-off homeland, he dwelt mentally on the peacefulness of the place.

> And I shall have some peace there, for peace comes
>   dropping slow,
> Dropping from the veils of the morning to where the cricket
>   sings.

He was called back home by a peacefulness best represented by a persistent sound:

> for always night and day
> I hear lake water lapping with low sound by the shore.

The word *lapping* reminds us that the tongue has other functions than that of speech. It is the organ of taste. Is it not perhaps the most remarkable thing about the human body that there are duplications of function for certain parts? There is no need to illustrate this point by dwelling on the astonishing duplication of function found in the sexual organs where the crude matter of drainage doubles with the delicate machinery of begetting and conceiving. For in the case of the tongue two rather refined and subtle functions are conjoined. The physical business of savoring and distinguishing the delicate flavors of what we eat and drink is itself a matter of great subtlety and refinement. The business of framing consonants and shaping vowels in rapid succession is also a matter requiring flexibility and versatility. I am no engineer, but I suspect that this duplication of functions so diverse is peculiar to God's works and differentiates them from man's. It seems to me that human engineering does not have this complexity. It is as though someone devised a new system of radar guidance for airplanes and then said, "Why not let the same instrumentation control the ovens that cook our food at home?" It is interesting that the psalmist calls us to "taste and see that the Lord is good"

(34:8), and St. Peter tells us that we may grow by nourishment of the word "if so be ye have tasted that the Lord is gracious" (1 Pt 2:3). And the two functions of the tongue in relation to speech and to food seem to come together in Psalm 119:103: "How sweet are thy words unto my taste."

TWENTY-SEVEN

Head

"**I** WOULD HAVE YOU KNOW," says St. Paul, "that the head of every man is Christ" (1 Cor 11:3). We are so accustomed to using the word *head* to suggest a controlling, governing factor that this comparison seems natural to us. If a man is "head" of a big business, then he directs its policy and oversees all its activities. It is in the head that the human brain is located. From here the whole organism is controlled. Damage a man's hand or his foot, and his activities may be curtailed, but you will not respect his judgment or his powers of direction any the less. Damage his head, and you may find that he can no longer function as a rational being. We use the word *head* sometimes merely for the area from which our hair grows, but perhaps more often for everything above the neck. When a man's head is cut off, it is severed at the neck. So we think of the head as containing the organs of sight, hearing, speech, and smell, the most subtle and sensitive of our physical faculties. As the area of the body also housing the brain and fronted by the face, it is naturally the part in which the whole personality is summed up and presented to the world. A portrait gallery or an illustrated book might contain as many pictures of heads and shoulders as of fully sketched men and women. But it would not contain studies of detached hands or feet unless it were a textbook in physiology.

Thus, if we pursue the metaphor of Christ as the head of

every man and woman, we arrive at a notion of a Christ who not only directs and controls a being, but also stamps his impress on that being, becoming the recognizable "personality" that confronts the world. This reasoning gives force to St. Paul's insistence that Christ "is the head of the body, the church" (Col 1:18), for God "hath put all things under his feet, and gave him to be the head over all things to the church" (Eph 1:22). He urges Christians to "grow up into him in all things, which is the head, even Christ" (Eph 4:15). All this imagery corroborates and enriches Christ's own application to himself of the psalmist's prophecy: "Did ye never read in the scriptures, The stone which the builders rejected, the same is become the head of the corner?" (Mt 21:42)

Christ as the head of his body, the church, and as head of every individual member of it is thus at once the cornerstone on which the stability of the whole human fabric is founded and sustained, and the governing power giving it eyes, ears, and speech, as well as the rational capacity to will and to do.

Something I heard of only last week has enriched for me the imagery of Christ as the head of his body, the church. It is some months since I wrote of heavy pre-spring rainfall in this area where I live. It is now August, the fourth month of one of the warmest and driest summers I have ever experienced. There is a two-hundred-year-old watermill not very far away. It has been restored to working life as part of the campaign to support organic farming and small-scale technology. It now produces 100 percent whole wheat flour, stone-ground from organically grown English wheat. The mill was built beside a stream which comes rushing down from a nearly three-thousand-foot mountain. The stream drops over two thousand feet within nine miles, and thus, with the help of a weir half a mile upstream, it rushes down the millrace with enough force to drive a couple of waterwheels twelve feet in diameter. The larger wheel develops fifteen horsepower. When some of my family visited this mill last week, they were told that, as a result of the prolonged drought, those operating the mill may soon, for the first time, face difficulties in keeping the machinery going. "The head of water may not be sufficient," the owners say. The head of water is the source of power for every process that takes place in the mill towards the making of bread. That Christ is our head is a powerful image. That Christ is the fountain of life-giving water is another powerful image. The image that combines the two, "the head of water," is a doubly powerful image. It includes the notion of vast resources of power sweeping down to operate the machinery of life. And we have not finished with the watermill imagery yet. For Christ is the bread of life, the 100 percent whole wheat bread of life. The head sends the baptismal waters sweeping down upon the wheels of our being so that we can grind the flour from which the bread of life is made to nourish ourselves and others.

The fact that the flour which makes the bread has been "stone-ground" is significant. I don't know much about the technology of milling, but the fact that flour has to be ground on stone is a significant one to the Christian for whom Christ is the headstone or cornerstone. The more closely the upper stone is balanced and the more heavily it weighs on the grain, the finer is the meal produced. Reduce the pressure, and the meal produced is coarser. One would not wish to press too literally the notion of Christ, the upper stone, bearing down upon our lives as we tumble about on the lower stone which is his human church. But the turning millstones certainly give us imagery reaching back to biblical times. We think perhaps too readily of the associations of the millstones with dead weight. And this is not surprising in view of our Lord's terrifying image: "It were better for him that a millstone were hanged about his neck, and he cast into the sea, than that he should offend one of these little ones" (Mt 18:6). But a millstone cast into the sea is a millstone disused. Imagery of millstones in productive use is more positive. When Jeremiah delivers one of the Lord's harsher judgments on those who are evil and go after other gods, he says: "I will take from them the voice of mirth, and the voice of gladness, the voice of the bridegroom, and the voice of the bride, the sound of the millstones, and the light of the candle" (Jer 25:10). Such is the recipe for desolation and misery: no laughter, no joy, no marriage blisses, no light to see by at night, no sound of turning millstones. The image recurs in the Book of Revelation. A mighty angel takes up a stone like a great millstone and casts it in the sea, saying: "Thus with violence shall that great city of Babylon be thrown down, and shall be found no more at all. And the voice of harpers, and musicians, and of pipers, and trumpeters, shall be heard no more at all in thee; and no craftsman, of whatever craft he be, shall be found any more in thee; and the sound of a millstone shall be heard no more at all in thee" (Rev 18:21-22).

> Though the mills of God grind slowly,
>   yet they grind exceeding small;
> Though with patience He stands waiting,
>   with exactness grinds He all.

So Longfellow wrote, and the lines have established themselves as a proverbial expression that the ways of Providence may be slow to manifest themselves, but nevertheless they have their effect on the minutest details of life. It is pleasant to set beside this concept the biblical image of the turning millstones which are a constant music in human ears, and to lack which would be a deprivation like the silencing of laughter, of joy, and of love.

We have moved some way from the "head of water" to the grinding millstones; but the interconnectedness of the whole process gives us a fine image of what life under God means; the process, that is, which starts with that vast reservoir of power gathered from the hills, whose waters are channeled down in a great torrent of energy to turn the wheels of productive human activity. The head is indeed a fountainhead. In days when watermills were common, such imagery sprang more naturally to mind. In Shakespeare's *Macbeth* King Duncan's two sons,

Malcolm and Donalbain, are roused from sleep by the noise of clanging bells and running feet and screaming voices. They come rushing downstairs to ask what the tumult is all about. "What is amiss?" they ask. And Macbeth reveals that their own father has been murdered:

> The spring, the head, the fountain of your blood
> Is stopped, the very source of it is stopped.

The head of water, the fountain of blood, has been dammed, plugged, dried up. The whole machinery of their lives is rendered virtually defunct. Christ is our spring, our head, our fountain; our head of water and our fountain of blood.

TWENTY-EIGHT

Crown

THE CROWN IS A SYMBOL of royalty, glory, and achievement. The act of putting a crown of gold upon the head as the mark of kingship has made "crowning" a way of recognizing supreme achievement. Expressions like "crown of gold" and "crown of glory" are scattered over our literature in general and over the Bible in particular. In Proverbs a "virtuous woman is a crown to her husband" (12:4); the psalmist calls for praise of the Lord because he "crowneth thee with loving-kindness and tender mercies" (Ps 103:4); again, when he praises God's blessing upon the earth in the fruits of the harvest, the psalmist says, "Thou crownest the year with thy goodness" (Ps 65:11). So all the richest blessings we receive, whether in the form of a loving wife, the personal gifts of Providence, or nature's grain and wine that nourish us, are seen in terms of our coronation. The act of crowning is at once a matter of showering blessings on the head and covering the head with glory. It is also a matter of consummating all other gifts in a uniquely supreme endowment.

Uniqueness is important. There are lots of subjects but there is only one king, only one queen. There are lots of runners but only one victor. A second and a third may win a silver and a bronze, but there is only one gold. There may be lots of nobility around a court, but there is only one monarch.

No one else would dare to be seen trying a crown on. This uniqueness of the crowned head is what makes the New Testament use of the image of the crown so startling. The image is charged with meaning. St. James's Epistle speaks of "the crown of life which the Lord hath promised to them that love him" (Jas 1:12), and in the Book of Revelation there is a ringing declaration: "Be thou faithful unto death, and I will give thee a crown of life" (Rev 2:10). Crowns, it seems, are being promised right and left. Indeed St. Paul roundly proclaims, "Henceforth there is laid up for me a crown of righteousness, which the Lord, the righteous judge, shall give me at that day; and not to me only, but unto all them also that love his appearing" (2 Tm 4:8).

Surely this is astonishing. The crown is the symbol of unique kingship, glorious achievement, lonely supremacy at the winning post. But the New Testament seems to be dishing out crowns to all and sundry. One hesitates to say they are "two a penny," for St. Paul leaves us in no doubt of the personal costliness of the long struggle against flesh and blood, against principalities and powers, that can alone equip one to claim the prize. Nevertheless crowns are available to "all them that love his appearing."

Biblical teaching is astonishing in that it lays the maximum stress on the glory and dignity of being crowned, the uniqueness of the man who is throned in sovereignty or wreathed in laurel for his record-breaking athletic prowess; and then it lays open the offer of the crown or laurel to all comers. There is a profound Christian truth hidden in the paradox. For in all earthly affairs effort and striving produce winners and losers, whether in the sports arena, the examination room, or the party convention. In all earthly affairs a victor can be proclaimed only at the expense of many, many losers. And you can get rid of the "inequality" between victors and losers only by abolishing victory. There are some areas of life where such is our passion for "equality," that we are in danger of abolishing victory. But not in all. It would be manifestly absurd for all the delegates at a party convention to emerge as front-runners for the presidency. The glory and the triumph of being chosen as party candidate depends absolutely and inevitably on the failure of thousands, indeed millions, of fellow human beings to be themselves elected. For every one person who wins a Nobel prize or an Olympic gold medal, who climbs Mount Everest or lands on the moon, there are millions who do not. In human terms, those failing millions are essential to the glory of the single winner. The rarity, the uniqueness of his achievement is what distinguishes him.

This contrast between the unique particularity of a triumph achieved and the ubiquity, by comparison, of nonachievement is bypassed in the Christian message. We can all be triumphant victors. We are all called to be triumphant victors. And the triumph will *not* take its glory from the knowledge that all around are losers who have failed. We find this hard to grasp. Just as we find it hard to grasp the notion of a life outside time in which there will be no past that is lost and no future that has yet to be realized, but an eternity in which all times are always present. Just as we are baffled by the notion of a divine mind who needs no yesterdays to make a today, so we are baffled by the notion of a divine mind that needs no failing millions to enhance the glory of the single victor, no throng of subjects and serfs to enhance the glory of the crowned sovereign. Similarly in God the knowledge of the whole in all its immensity does not detract from the knowledge of every minuscule part in all its diminutiveness. Our Lord himself made the point. The Maker of the galaxies knows every sparrow. "But even the very hairs of your head are all numbered" (Lk 12:7).

On earth, of course, Christ the King was not crowned with a golden crown but with a crown of thorns. His victory was a conquest in suffering, and his crown testified to that. His lordship required the overturning of all earthly kingships based on greed, oppression, and pride, and to that extent he could be crowned on earth only in parody. Or shall we put it the other way round? That all corrupt earthly kingships have been but parodic mockeries of what the sovereignty of Christ stands for. It has been on the lips of Christian teachers and preachers throughout the centuries that the crown of thorns has to be received and worn before the crown of glory can be granted.

This does not mean that all earthly authority stands in opposition to divine authority. There have always been good kings and bad kings, good rulers and bad rulers. It is interesting to note, at the end of our consideration of the images of the head and the crown, that kings and emperors, and indeed dukes and lesser rulers, have had the image of their heads stamped on their coinage as a guarantee of its validity. Very often they have been crowned heads. It is within living memory that our British currency included "crowns" and "half-crowns." They were once silver. And the crown was a quarter the value of a "sovereign," which was gold. We know from Shakespeare that earlier coinage included "nobles" and "ducats" (from "duchy"). This dignifying of the means of exchange with the authoritative stamp of a ruler was a guarantee of authenticity. Christ himself drew attention to Caesar's image on the coinage of his own time. Coinage was thus a powerful symbol of royal authority in action. John Donne wrote a poem to a friend, Mr. Tilman, who had accepted a vocation to the priesthood and had just been ordained.

> Thou art the same materials as before,
> Only the stamp is changed; but no more.

Donne explains how a new king keeps the old coinage used by his predecessor but has a new face stamped on it. In the same way the old image of God was stamped on Mr. Tilman by creation, but grace has replaced this with the new image of Christ:

      so hath grace
Changed only God's old Image by Creation
To Christ's new stamp at this thy Coronation.

The act of giving himself to God's service in the priesthood is a "coronation," and it is marked by the stamping of Christ's image on the old coinage of his former life.

What is interesting to us about such trains of thought is that the Christian mind could see even money as something which could be regarded as appropriate imagery of God's earthly activity among us. Coinage achieves authenticity by the image of the sovereign stamped upon it. But coinage sometimes carried religious symbols too. There was a coin known as an "angel" in medieval England, and in Victorian England the two-sovereign piece carried the image of St. George slaying the dragon. Now it may be a good thing not to cheapen religious symbols by overuse of them in the wrong context. One cannot think that it would be a good idea to have our dollar bills or pound notes bearing the image of the crucified Savior. Nevertheless the desire to give our means of exchange a mark of the sacred was a healthy one. Money is the direct means by which most of us obtain the good things of life that nourish our families and ourselves. The urge to sacralize it, to mark it as something that plays a crucial part in our life under God, is surely healthy. In an age when we suffer so much from the desacralization of human life—whether it be of love, marriage, parenthood, or whatever—it is salutary to remember how Christendom has sometimes given even its money a role in interpreting the sacred in terms of the mundane.

TWENTY-NINE

Bride

THE IMAGE OF THE CHURCH as the bride of Christ derives from the Book of Revelation. There the saved are gathered in the new Jerusalem, the home of the blessed, and a double correspondence emerges. John sees "the holy city, new Jerusalem, coming down from God out of heaven, prepared as a bride adorned for her husband" (Rev 21:2). As the vision continues, John is carried away by an angel who says, "Come hither, I will shew thee the bride, the Lamb's wife" (Rev 21:9), and the beauty and glory of the city are described in detail. In poetic terms there is perhaps no more exciting image than this in the whole of Christian literature. One of the most popular hymns of English-speaking Christendom begins:

The Church's one foundation
Is Jesus Christ her Lord;
She is his new creation
By water and the word;
From heaven he came and sought her
To be his holy Bride;
With his own blood he bought her,
And for her life he died.

It is not surprising that, throughout the ages, marriage sermons have been preached which see human unions in terms of this correspondence. In one of John Donne's marriage sermons he declares: "So in this spiritual marriage we consider first Christ and his Church for the persons; but more particularly, Christ and my soul." The human union which is seen in general terms as reflecting the bond between Christ and his beloved church for whom he died, is seen in particular terms as reflecting the bond between Christ and each individually beloved human soul for whom he died.

In this parallel each human soul is seen as feminine in relation to Christ's masculinity. The Victorian poet, Coventry Patmore, toyed a great deal with the idea that the love of man for woman is an image of the love of God for the human soul. He did indeed indulge some risky parallels in pursuing this theme. The human soul's reluctance to surrender itself to God's personal claim upon it has that kind of vanity and self-protectiveness which modest femininity is traditionally supposed to involve. We are all (men and women alike) like brides sought and cherished by the divine Spouse and holding off in falsely demure self-protectiveness. Thus the poet pictures a beautiful maiden who rouses sick longings for marriage in her suitor, and then he addresses the young man thus:

> What if this Lady be thy Soul, and He
> Who claims to enjoy her sacred beauty be,
> Not thou, but God; and thy sick fire
> A female vanity,
> Such as a Bride, viewing her mirror'd charms,
> Feels when she sighs, "all these are for his arms!"

We may find the Victorian bedroom scene a little dated, not to say cloying, but Patmore's parallels remain essentially valid.

He pushed these parallels to daring lengths. In a prose passage in his book, *The Rod, the Root, and the Flower*, he writes, "The Bride is always 'Amoris Victima' (the sacrificial Victim of Love)" and he sees God's descent into human flesh in Christ as a divine act of union like the consummation of a marriage. In the crucifixion the human flesh thus entered, creation thus invaded, heaves a great cry like the bride at consummation.

> The real and innnermost sacrifice of the Cross was the consummation of the descent of Divinity into the flesh and its identification therewith; and the sigh which all creation heaved in that moment has its echo in that of mortal love in the like descent. That sigh is the inmost heart of all music.

Living as we do in a permissive age that tends to reduce everything human to its crude naturalistic level, it may be that we are nowadays too squeamish about sexual love in its really momentous aspects to be able to stomach the bold and powerful imagery of a Victorian poet; but comparable imagery has been explored in all ages.

In *Paradise Lost* Milton describes Eve in her beauty and innocence in words which sometimes delicately echo St. John's description of the bride of Christ, the new Jerusalem, in particular by repetitive use of the word *adorned*. (It may be noted here in parenthesis that English poetry from Milton to T.S. Eliot has relied so often for its significant overtones on echoing words and phrases from the Bible that unfamiliarity with the King James Version strips important passages of their true meaning. That is one reason why the King James Bible is quoted throughout this book.) The first human marriage is naturally presented by Milton as the historical human arche-type of all subsequent marriages. It is also therefore in line with the marriage between Christ and his church which is the spiritual archetype of all human marriages.

The Christian doctrine of grace teaches us that in all positive impulses of spiritual life and in all human acts of virtue God is always the initiator. He plants the seed in us that grows and flowers. In this sense the human soul is feminine in relation to divine masculinity. The love of God for men and women is prior to the love of men and women for God. Men and women are always in their acts of worship and love responsive to what God himself has initiated. Small wonder that in all ages Christian marriage has been seen in terms of the human soul's union with the God who has wooed it, in terms of the virgin soul's full surrender of itself to impregnation by the divine. This is the pattern of all earthly fruitfulness.

We have reached the stage of civilization in which marriage is often regarded as a private pact between two individuals to throw in their lots together, and in so far as this relationship is "institutionalized" it is accepted as a convenient social arrangement for establishing partnerships on an advantageous socioeconomic basis. There is a movement at work to desacralize marraige, to empty it of its transcendental dimensions. It is a betrayal of Christian principles to think of marriage in purely human terms. It is a betrayal of Christian principles to think of falling in love in purely human terms. And it is a betrayal of Christian principles to think of male and female in purely human terms. That is why it is nonsense to pretend that the essential masculine and feminine roles can be interchanged or the masculine-feminine differentiation blurred or ironed out. For the pattern of roles and relationships established by the traditional concept of sexual polarities and sustained in the traditional conventions of wooing and mating reduplicates living principles of the natural world and of supernatural life.

The human partner in the union which produced the incarnate Son of God was feminine. We have already referred to imagery which presents woman as man's garden or woman as the earth which nourishes the seed and brings forth fruit. Such imagery is not reversible. If you conceive of the fruitfulness of marriage as totally distinct in principle from the fruitfulness of nature or the fruitfulness of God's grace, you are not living mentally in God's world. For the pattern of relationships between the sexes, the rhythmic balance between initiation and response, between wooing and yielding, between husbanding and mothering, between planting the seed and bringing forth the fruit, is deeply ingrained in the life of nature on the one hand and in the pattern of God's ways with humanity on the other hand.

To live mentally in God's world is to recognize an interrelationship between the human, the natural, and the divine which threads its way through all creation. That is what the doctrine of the Incarnation is all about. Incarnation is the bridal of the human and the divine.

THIRTY

Word

SOME BIBLICAL COMMENTATORS tend to imply that there is something very subtle and remarkable in the Old Testament use of such expressions as "the word of the Lord," which conveys the idea of a divine message or a divine act that is charged with momentousness. They are at pains to point out that there is a far more profound connection between God and his word in such contexts than there would be between me and my word if someone asked me what I wanted for tea and I said, "Crumpets." But our ordinary human conversation has many expressions which infuse a great wealth of meaning into the connection between a person and his word. When you say of someone that he is a person whose word can be trusted, you do not mean by that that when he says, "Crumpets" you can be quite sure he does not mean "Boiled eggs." You rather pay a tribute to his general integrity. You say that he is a man of his word, and the notion of single words like *crumpets* or *eggs* is swallowed up in a tribute to all-round honesty and uprightness.

So there is a hint of moral integrity, of utter faithfulness, about our use of the noun *word* in many specifically human contexts. "His word is his bond," we say. "Upon my word" used to be a forceful guarantee like "I give you my word." "Take my word for it" is another guarantee of authenticity. "He will be as good as his word" implies that he will live up to a perhaps exacting standard. "You can take him at his word" testifies to a person's genuineness. As well as these associations with honesty and reliability, usages of the noun *word* also have associations with authority and firmness. To "say the word" is to give the signal of command that sets something in motion. The "word of command" suggests the maximum in trustworthy integrity. To "speak a word in season" and to "have a good word for someone or something" are expressions for positive helpfulness. Indeed it is difficult to think of popular idiomatic usages of the noun *word* (in the singular and without qualifying adjective) that are not colored by associations of quality and approval. *Word* tends to be connotatively a "good" word.

Yet the human associations of honesty, reliability, and authority, which readily accrue to connotations of the noun *word,* are a comparatively minor matter in estimating the powerful significance that the noun has for Christians. It is a remarkable fact that of all the words richly utilized in Christian teaching and writing no word is more richly utilized than *word* itself. A little thought will reveal that *word* is different from most other words. It does not make much sense (except in a highly poetic or fanciful way) to say, "A man is a man," or, "A hammer is a hammer," for you do not convey anything by these repetitions. But it certainly makes a point to say that *word* is a word, as it would make a point to say that *man* is a word. The italics make a difference. For though *man* is a word, a man is certainly not a word. The game we play with italics becomes obvious to everyone if I say, quite correctly, that *verb* is a noun.

In a sense this book has been devoted to words. And it is itself, like all books, a collection of words. A collection of words about words. But you might well object to this claim as being a false simplification. You might reply: "Not at all. When you wrote under the heading 'Fire,' you did not talk about a collection of four letters, *F, I, R, E,* combined in a way derived from the Anglo-Saxon word *fyr*; you talked about coals blazing in a hearth. Your book would really have been about words only if you had written as a philologist or semanticist." Should I have to accept this correction and agree that only an expert in some branch of linguistics could write a book about words? I think not. Suppose you press your point and say: "You have not been writing about words as such; you have not been writing about words as words; you have been writing about what words convey." Surely I can reply that to disregard what words convey is the very opposite of treating words as words, for they are essentially conveyors of meaning. That is their raison d'etre. Words exist to convey meaning as roofs exist to keep the rain off. If you treat words as though the essential thing about them were that they are monosyllabic or bisyllabic, nouns or verbs, derived from Latin or from Anglo-Saxon, developed in this way or in that, you ignore the very essence of words, the thing that make them what they are, conveyors of meaning.

There is a sense in which *word* is the emptiest of all words, for it directs the mind to nothing outside itself. (It is itself a specimen of what it means.)There is a sense in which *word* is the richest of all words, for it directs the mind to the vehicle by which all meaning is conveyed, all rational thought expressed, all articulate feeling voiced. There is a paradoxically unlimited resesrvoir of power hidden in the word *word*. On the surface it refers to nothing outside the world of its own substance as a collection of letters on a page or sounds in the air. By contrast, the word *garden,* say, takes you mentally right outside the world of the printed page into a world of color and light packed with beautiful living and growing things. And the word *airplane* takes you mentally into a world of machinery, a world of cabins, flight decks, roaring takeoffs, floating stillness over a carpet of clouds, and shuddering landings. While the word *word* takes you back on to itself as a collection of letters, colorless and substanceless.

But . . . but . . . precisely because *garden* is a word and *airplane* is a word, this thing *word* can take you on a journey amid tokens that represent together all objects, all concepts, all dreams, that were ever experienced or entertained by the human mind. The word *word* capsulates within itself in summary a reference to every thought and feeling communicatively uttered by men and women since the world began. Thus you have only to say "word" and you have sparked off a current that could run its course through everything ever experienced, fashioned, or conceived by the human mind. Small wonder that, though you can say, "*Man* is a word," or, "*Garden* is a word," you cannot say, "A man is a word," or "A garden is a word." But you can say, "*Christ* is a word," and then say, "Christ is the Word." *The* Word, not *a* word. The vehicle of all meaning. The key to all meaning. The impulse that sets a current of connotation running its course through every experience, act, or thought known to humankind. It is the universality of the word *word* that makes it so powerful an image of Christ. The fact that it makes contact with everything that the human race has ever done or known. The fact that it sends a current coursing through the network of all things earthly and human to touch every object, deed, and thought with its claim of relevance. The network extends over the universal. Is it a house, a tree, a woman, a picture, a dream, an argument, a theory, a flight, a kangaroo? It may be any of these, but as soon as it is grasped, uttered, and communicated by the human being, it is also a word. Here at the center of human conceiving and doing stands the single inescapable basis of relationship, significance, and unity—the word.

We accept that *word,* in its most limited and literal reference, pulls our thoughts upon itself as a form that appears in print or is heard in utterance, but stops short of touching the living experience of any but the lexicographer, the grammarian, the philologist, and the semanticist in their professional capacities. But when *word* is made flesh in this word or that word, then any living experience of men and women of any kind and in any age may be touched and comprehended.

It is through words that we can conceive and discuss the

difference between standing and walking, between a flower and an animal, between beauty and ugliness, between good and evil. Whenever such distinctions are made, words take on the business of rendering experience meaningful and interpretable. We can conceive of rational human life without planes or even wheels, without cities or even buildings; but we cannot imagine rational human life without words. Small wonder that St. John found here the key image of Christ's impact upon the human world. "All things were made by him" as the Word, and all life is rendered meaningful for us by the Word. "The Word was made flesh and dwelt among us." By the word in action and through the Word made flesh the glory of all things is revealed to us.